Interlude

BY KNIT PICKS

Photography by John Cranford

Printed in the United States of America

First Printing, 2019

ISBN 978-1-62767-221-4

Versa Press, Inc.

800-447-7829

www.versapress.com

CONTENTS

Give yourself
the permission ...

AAMU

by Joanna Ignatius

FINISHED MEASUREMENTS
34.5 (38.25, 42.25, 46.25, 48, 51.25, 54, 60, 64)" finished bust measurement; garment is meant to be worn with 2-4" of positive ease

YARN
Knit Picks Alpaca Cloud (fingering weight, 100% Superfine Alpaca; 200 yards/50g): Sophia 26912, 4 (5, 5, 6, 6, 7, 8, 8, 9) hanks
Knit Picks Aloft (lace weight, 72% Super Kid Mohair, 28% Silk; 260 yards/25g): White 25213, 4 (4, 4, 5, 5, 6, 7, 7, 8) balls

NEEDLES
US 10 (6mm) 32" circular needles and DPNs, or one 32" or longer circular needle for Magic Loop technique, or size to obtain gauge

US 9 (5.5mm) 24" circular needle for neck finishing, or one size smaller than size used to obtain gauge

NOTIONS
Yarn Needle
Stitch Markers
Scrap Yarn

GAUGE
16 sts and 20 rows = 4" in stockinette stitch in the round with yarns held together, blocked

Aamu

Notes:

Aamu is a long, loose, slightly A-lined raglan sweater worked seamlessly from the top down in the round, with the two yarns held together throughout. First the top of the neck and sleeves are worked flat, then stitches are cast on to continue to knit the body in the round. After separating the sleeves, gradually widening garter stitch wedges are worked from the underarm. The bottom back is shaped with short rows to create a longer back. After finishing the body, the sleeves are knitted in the round. Last, the neckline is finished with garter stitch.

Aamu is Finnish and means morning. Wearing Aamu is like wrapping yourself with a soft, fluffy cloud that keeps you comfy and warm all day long.

Stockinette Stitch (St st, worked flat over any number of sts)
Row 1 (RS): Knit all sts.
Row 2 (WS): Purl all sts.
Rep Rows 1 and 2 for pattern.
To work St st in the rnd, K every rnd.

Garter Stitch (in the rnd over any number of sts)
Rnd 1: Purl all sts.
Rnd 2: Knit all sts.
Rep Rnds 1 and 2 for pattern.

M1L (Make 1 Left-leaning st)
PU the bar between st just worked and next st, place on LH needle as a regular st; K TBL.

M1R (Make 1 Right-leaning st)
PU the bar between st just worked and next st, place on LH needle backwards (incorrect st mount); K TFL.

German Short Rows
K or P to the st indicated in the pattern, turn. Slide the last worked st from LH needle to RH needle. Bring yarn up, over and back and pull tightly so that the slipped st slides around and there are two legs visible (i.e. it forms a double st). Continue to K or P as indicated in pattern. When you resume work in the rnd, K the double wrapped st as if it was one st.

Stretchy Bind Off (for hem and cuffs)
K2 sts. *SL both sts back to the LH needle, K the 2 sts TBL, K1. Rep from * to the end until 1 st is left, break yarn and pull end through the last loop.

DIRECTIONS
Setup and Raglan Increases
With larger needle and both yarns held together, CO 48 (50, 52, 54, 54, 56, 56, 60, 60) sts.
Row 1 (WS): P2, PM for Front, P2, PM for Raglan, P4 (4, 4, 4, 4, 4, 4, 6, 6), PM for Sleeve, P2, PM for Raglan, P28 (30, 32, 34, 34, 36, 36, 36, 36), PM for Back, P2, PM for Raglan, P4 (4, 4, 4, 4, 4, 4, 6, 6), PM for Sleeve, P2, PM for Raglan, P2 Front sts.

Row 2 (RS): K to M, M1R, SM, K2, SM, M1L, K to M, M1R, SM, K2, SM, M1L, K to M, M1R, SM, K2, SM, M1L, K to M, M1R, SM, K2, SM, M1L, K to end. 8 sts inc.
Row 3 (WS): P all sts.
Row 4 Sizes 35, 39, 43, 47, 49, 52" Only (RS): K to M, M1R, SM, K2, SM, K to M, SM, K2, SM, M1L, K to M, M1R, SM, K2, SM, K to M, SM, K2, SM, M1L, K to end. 4 sts inc.
Row 4 Sizes 55, 61, 65" Only (RS): K to M, M1R, SM, K2, SM, M1L, K to M, M1R, SM, K2, SM, M1L, K to M, M1R, SM, K2, SM, M1L, K to M, M1R, SM, K2, SM, M1L, K to end. 8 sts inc.
Row 5 (WS): P all sts.

All Sizes
Work Rows 2-5 twice more. 8 sts for each front, 2 sts for each raglan seam, 10 (10, 10, 10, 10, 10, 16, 18, 18) sts for each sleeve, 40 (42, 44, 46, 46, 48, 48, 48, 48) sts for back, 84 (86, 88, 90, 90, 92, 104, 108, 108) total sts.
Row 6 (RS): K1, M1R, K to M, M1R, SM, K2, SM, M1L, K to M, M1R, SM, K2, SM, M1L, K to M, M1R, SM, K2, SM, M1L, K to M, M1R, SM, K2, SM, M1L, K to 1 st before end, M1L, K1. 10 sts inc.
Row 7 (WS): P all sts
Row 8 Sizes 39, 43, 47" Only (RS): K1, M1R, K to M, M1R, SM, K2, SM, K to M, SM, K2, SM, M1L, K to M, M1R, SM, K2, SM, K to M, SM, K2, SM, M1L, K to 1 st before end, M1L, K1. 6 sts inc.
Row 8 Sizes 35, 49, 52, 55, 61, 65" Only (RS): K1, M1R, K to M, M1R, SM, K2, SM, M1L, K to M, M1R, SM, K2, SM, M1L, K to M, M1R, SM, K2, SM, M1L, K to M, M1R, SM, K2, SM, M1L, K to 1 st before end, M1L, K1. 10 sts inc.
Row 9 (WS): P1, M1R P-wise, K to 1 st before end, M1L P-wise, P1. 2 sts inc.
Row 10 (RS): K1, M1R, K to M, M1R, SM, K2, SM, M1L, K to M, M1R, SM, K2, SM, M1L, K to M, M1R, SM, K2, SM, M1L, K to M, M1R, SM, K2, SM, M1L, K to 1 st before end, M1L, K1, CO 16 (18, 20, 22, 22, 24, 24, 24, 24) sts, PM (beginning of rnd) and join to work in the rnd. 46 (48, 50, 52, 52, 54, 54, 54, 54) sts for each front and back, 2 sts for each raglan seam, 16 (14, 14, 14, 16, 22, 24, 24) sts for each sleeve, 116 (118, 122, 126, 128, 132, 138, 140, 140) total sts.
Begin working in the rnd.
Rnd 1: K all sts.
Rnd 2: (K to M, M1R, SM, K2, SM, M1L) x3, K to end, SM. 8 sts inc.
Rep the last two rnds 7 (10, 13, 16, 17, 20, 21, 18, 15) more times. 62 (70, 78, 86, 88, 96, 98, 92, 86) sts for each front and back, 2 sts for each raglan seam, 32 (36, 42, 48, 52, 58, 66, 62, 56) sts for each sleeve. 196 (220, 248, 276, 288, 316, 336, 316, 292) sts.

Sizes 43, 47, 49, 52, and 55" Only
Work Rnd 1 once more.

Sizes 35 (39)" Only
Rnd 1: K all sts
Rnd 2: K to M, SM, K2, SM, M1L, K to M, M1R, SM, K2, SM, K to M, SM, K2, SM, M1R, K to M, M1L, SM, K2, SM, K to end. 4 sts inc.
Rep the last two rnds 2 (1) more times. Work 1 Rnd in St st.

Sizes 61 (65)" Only

Rnd 1: K to M, M1R, SM, K2, SM, K to M, SM, K2, SM, M1L, K to M, M1R, SM, K2, SM, K to M, SM, K2, SM, M1L, K to end, SM. 4 sts inc.

Rnd 2: (K to M, M1R, SM, K2, SM, M1L) x3, K to end, SM. 8 sts inc.

Rep the last 2 rnds 3 (7) more times. Work 1 Rnd in St st. 62 (70, 78, 86, 88, 96, 98, 108, 118) sts for each front and back, 2 sts for each raglan seam, 38 (40, 42, 48, 52, 58, 66, 70, 72) sts for each sleeve. 208 (228, 248, 276, 288, 316, 336, 364, 388) sts.

Separate the Sleeves

Next Rnd: K to M, remove M, K1, SL the next 40 (42, 44, 50, 54, 60, 68, 72, 74) sts onto a holder (remove Ms as you come to them), PM (new beginning of rnd M), CO 6 (6, 6, 6, 8, 6, 10, 12, 10) sts, PM, K1, remove M, K to M, remove M, K1, SL the next 40 (42, 44, 50, 54, 60, 68, 72, 74) sts on a holder (remove Ms as you come to them), PM, CO 6 (6, 6, 6, 8, 6, 10, 12, 10) sts, PM, K to M, remove M, K to the new beginning of rnd M. 140 (156, 172, 188, 196, 208, 220, 244, 260) sts.

Body

Cont to work in the rnd. If you want a shorter body, work one or more of the First Inc sets and fewer of the Second Inc sets.

First Inc Set

Rnds 1, 3: K all sts.

Rnds 2, 4: SM, P to M, SM, K to M, SM, P to M, SM, K to end of rnd.

Rnd 5: SM, M1R, K to M, M1L, SM, K to M, SM, M1R, K to M, M1L, SM, K to end of rnd. 4 sts inc, 2 in each Garter panel.

Rnd 6: Rep Rnd 2.

Rep the last 6 rnds 4 more times. 160 (176, 192, 208, 216, 228, 240, 264, 280) sts.

Second Inc Set

Rnds 1, 3, 5, 7, 9: K all sts.

Rnds 2, 4, 6, 8, 10: SM, P to M, SM, K to M, SM, P to M, SM, K to end of rnd.

Rnd 11: SM, M1R, K to M, M1L, SM, K to M, SM, M1R, K to M, M1L, SM, K to end of rnd. 4 sts inc.

Rnd 12: SM, Rep Rnd 2.

Rep the last 12 rnds 4 more times. 180 (196, 212, 228, 236, 248, 260, 284, 300) sts.

Knit 1 rnd even.

If you want more length to the body, work more rows even in pattern as established before starting the short rows.

Short Row 1 (RS): SM, P to M, K to M, W&T.

Short Row 2 (WS): P to M, W&T.

Short Row 3 (RS): K to 4 sts before previous turn, W&T.

Short Row 4 (WS): P to 4 sts before previous turn, W&T.

Rep Short Rows 3 and 4 one more time.

Resume working in the rnd. K to M working the wrapped sts as one st, SM, P to M, SM, K to M, SM, K to M, SM, K to M working the wrapped sts as one st, K to end of rnd.

Hem

Work in garter stitch for 15 rnds.
BO all sts using the Stretchy Bind Off.

Sleeves (make 2 the same)

Transfer held 40 (42, 44, 50, 54, 60, 68, 72, 74) sleeve
sts onto DPNs or circular needle ready for working a small
circumference in the rnd. Starting in the center of underarm
CO, PU and K 3 (3, 3, 3, 4, 3, 5, 6, 5) sts, K sleeve sts, PU and
K 3 (3, 3, 3, 4, 3, 5, 6, 5) sts, PM. 46 (48, 50, 56, 62, 66, 78,
84, 84) sts.
Rnd 1: K1, K2tog, K to 3 sts before end, SSK, K1. 44 (46, 48,
54, 60, 64, 76, 82, 82) sts.

Work in the rnd in St st for 2.5" from underarm CO.
Dec Rnd: K1, K2tog, K to 3 sts before end, SSK, K1. 2 sts dec.
*Work in St st for 3.5 (3.5, 3.5, 2.5, 1.75, 1.5, 1, 0.75, 0.75)" then
work another Dec Rnd. Rep from * 2 (2, 2, 4, 6, 7, 13, 16, 15)
more times. 36 (38, 40, 42, 44, 46, 46, 46, 48) sts.
Work in St st until sleeve measures 20", or 2" shorter than
desired length.

Cuff

Work in Garter stitch for 15 rnds.
BO all sts using the Stretchy Bind Off.

Neck

With smaller circular needle and RS facing, starting from
the right raglan seam, PU and K 3 (3, 3, 3, 3, 3, 3, 5, 5) sts
from the sleeve, PU and K 22 (24, 26, 28, 28, 29, 29, 29, 29)
sts across back, PU and K 3 (3, 3, 3, 3, 3, 3, 5, 5) sts from the
sleeve, PU and K 12 sts from the front, PU and K 14 (16, 18, 20,
20, 22, 22, 22, 22) sts from the neckline CO, PU and K 12 sts
from the front, PM. 66 (70, 74, 78, 78, 81, 81, 85, 85) sts.
Work in Garter stitch for 5 rnds.
BO all sts.

Finishing

Weave in ends, wash, and block to diagram.

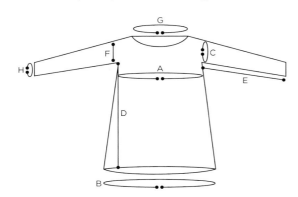

A: 35 (39, 43, 47, 49, 52, 55, 61, 65)"
B: 45 (49, 53, 57, 59, 62, 65, 71, 75)"
C: 11 (11.5, 12, 13.5, 15, 16, 19, 20.5, 20.5)"
D: Front Length Underarm to Hem: 21.5"
   Back Length Underarm to Hem: 23.25"
E: 22"
F: 6.5 (7.25, 7.75, 9, 9.25, 10.5, 10.75, 11.25, 11.5)"
G: 16.5 (17.5, 18.5, 19.5, 19.5, 20.25, 20.25, 21.5, 21.5)"
H: 9 (9.5, 10, 10.5, 11, 11.5, 11.5, 11.5, 12)"

BRIOCHE WRAPPER

by Quenna Lee

FINISHED MEASUREMENTS

48.75 (52, 57.25, 60.5)″ finished bust circumference; garment is meant to be worn with 10-16″ of positive ease

YARN

Knit Picks Simply Alpaca (Aran weight, 100% Superfine Alpaca; 246 yards/100g): Alfie 27490, 4 (5, 5, 5) hanks

NEEDLES

US 8 (5mm) 24″ or longer circular needles, or size to obtain gauge
US 7 (4.5mm) 16″ circular needle, or one size smaller than size used to obtain gauge

NOTIONS

Yarn Needle
Stitch Markers
Scrap Yarn or Stitch Holder
Spare DPNs

GAUGE

18 sts and 32 rows = 4″ in Half-Brioche pattern on larger needles, blocked
16 sts and 32 rows = 4″ in garter stitch on larger needles, blocked

Brioche Wrapper

Notes:

Echoes of wintery days filled with warm hot chocolate linger in the soft lines of this draped, shawl-like cardigan. This wrapper seamlessly blends memories of home comforts with an air of simple elegance. The Brioche Wrapper is worked in three pieces. The fronts and shawl collar are worked at the same time before seaming into a long rectangular shape. The back is worked from the bottom up, back and forth. To construct the wrapper, the back is seamed to the fronts and the edges are seamed to the front, leaving an opening for the armholes.

Since the recommended yarn lengthens after blocking, unblocked vertical measurements are slightly shorter than the blocked measurements. After pieces are finished, they are blocked to the schematic measurements.

Note: wrapper can be worn with the band at the top as a collar or at the bottom as a hem.

SL1YOF
SL next st P-wise WYIF, yarn over needle to back, then between needles to front.

Brioche Purl (BRP)
Purl st tog with its companion YO.

Half-Brioche (worked flat over an even number of sts)
Row 1 (RS): *SL1YOF, P1; rep from * to end.
Row 2 (WS): *K1, BRP; rep from * to end.
Rep Rows 1-2 for pattern.

3-Needle Bind Off
A tutorial for the 3-Needle Bind Off can be found at https://tutorials.knitpicks.com/3-needle-bind-off/.

DIRECTIONS
Right Front
With larger needle, CO 55 (59, 65, 69) sts.
Set-up Row (WS): SL1, *K1, P1; rep from * to last 8 sts, K1, PM, K to end.
Row 1 (RS): SL1, K to M, SM, P1, work Half-Brioche pattern to last st, K1.
Row 2 (WS): SL1, work Half-Brioche pattern to 1 st before M, K1, SM, K to end.
Rep last 2 rows until piece measures 13" from CO, ending with a WS row.

Shape Right Front Band
Inc Row (RS): SL1, K to M, M1, SM, cont pattern as established to end. 1 st inc.
Rep Inc Row every 10th row 7 more times. 63 (67, 73, 77) sts.
Work in pattern until piece measures 25 (26, 27, 28)" from CO, ending with a WS row. Place sts on holder.

Left Front
With larger needle, CO 55 (59, 65, 69) sts.
Set-up Row (WS): SL1, K6, PM, *K1, P1; rep from * to last 2 sts, K2.
Row 1 (RS): SL1, P1, work Half-brioche pattern to M, SM, K to end.
Row 2 (WS): SL1, K to M, SM, work Half-Brioche pattern to last 2 sts, K2.
Rep Rows 1-2 until piece measures 13" from CO, ending with WS row.

Shape Left Front Band

Inc Row (RS): Work in pattern as established to M, SM, M1, K to end. 1 st inc.

Rep Inc Row every 10th row 7 more times. 63 (67, 73, 77) sts. Work in pattern until piece measures 25 (26, 27, 28)" from CO, ending with a WS row.

With 3-Needle BO, seam Left and Right Fronts together.

Back

With larger needles, CO 109 (117, 127, 135) sts.

Set-up Row (WS): SL1, *K1, P1; rep from * to last 2 sts, K2.

Row 1 (RS): SL1, P1, work Half-Brioche pattern to last st, K1.

Row 2 (WS): SL1, work Half-Brioche pattern to last 2 sts, K2

Cont in pattern until piece measures 13", ending with a WS row.

BO as follows: Sl1, BO in (P1, K1) pattern to end.

Finishing

Weave in ends. Block pieces to schematic measurements. Seam BO back edge to the center of front (non-band side). Seam the vertical edges of back to corresponding front piece from the hem up for 7 (6.5, 6, 5.5)" or until armhole opening measures 8 (8.5, 9, 9.5)" when flat. See schematic for specifics.

Armhole Edging (make 2 the same)

With smaller needle, beginning at bottom of armhole, PU and K 72 (78, 82, 86) sts evenly around armhole edge. PM, and join to work in the rnd.

Next Rnd: *K1, P1; rep from * to end.

Work 3 rnds even as established.

BO all sts in pattern.

Weave in ends.

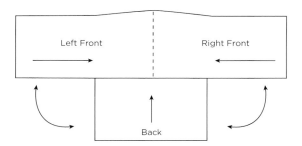

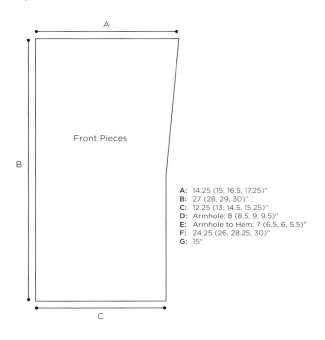

A: 14.25 (15, 16.5, 17.25)"
B: 27 (28, 29, 30)"
C: 12.25 (13, 14.5, 15.25)"
D: Armhole: 8 (8.5, 9, 9.5)"
E: Armhole to Hem: 7 (6.5, 6, 5.5)"
F: 24.25 (26, 28.25, 30)"
G: 15"

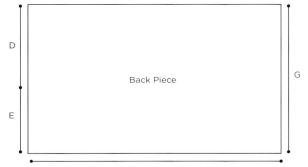

CASSIDY

by Maria Leigh

FINISHED MEASUREMENT

36.75 (40, 43.25, 46.5, 49.5, 52.75)″ finished bust circumference, meant to be worn with 6″ of positive ease

YARN

Knit Picks Color Mist (worsted weight, 75% Pima Cotton, 25% Acrylic; 219 yards/100g): Tidewater 27465, 5 (5, 6, 6, 7, 8) hanks

NEEDLES

US 7 (4.5mm) DPNs plus 32″ and 16″ circular needles, or size to obtain gauge

US 6 (4.mm) DPNs plus 32″ and 16″ circular needles, or one size smaller than size used to obtain gauge

NOTIONS

Yarn Needle
Stitch Markers
Spare Needles or Scrap Yarn

GAUGE

20 sts and 26 rnds = 4″ stockinette stitch in the rnd on larger needles, blocked

Cassidy

Notes:

Cassidy is a top-down raglan pullover worked in the round.

PS: Purl Seam (the raglan seam on the Yoke section, and the faux side seams on the Body and Sleeve sections).

1x1 Rib (worked in the round over an even number of sts)
All Rnds: *K1, P1; rep from * to end of rnd.

Wrap and Turn (W&T)
A tutorial for the Wrap and Turn (W&T) can be found at http://tutorials.knitpicks.com/wptutorials/short-rows-wrap -and-turn-or-wt/.

DIRECTIONS
Yoke
Loosely CO 112 sts with smaller needle. Join to work in the rnd. PM, being careful to not twist sts.
Knit all for 3 Rnds.
Work 1x1 Rib for 4 rnds, remove M. K1 (0, 1, 0, 1, 0), PM.
Switch to larger needle.

Shoulder Shaping
Setup Rnd: K20, (21, 22, 23, 24, 25), P1, K13 (11, 9, 7, 5, 3), P1, K43 (45, 47, 49, 51, 53), P1, K13 (11, 9, 7, 5, 3), P1, K19 (20, 21, 22, 23, 24). 39 (41, 43, 45, 57, 49) sts for back, 43 (45, 47, 49, 51, 53) sts for front, 13 (11, 9, 7, 5, 3) for each sleeve, and a single purl st for each PS. First st of rnd is at center st of back. 112 sts.
Short Row 1 (RS): K16 (17, 18, 19, 20, 21), W&T.
Short Row 2 (WS): P16 (17, 18, 19, 20, 21), SM, P15 (16, 17, 18, 19, 20), W&T.
Short Row 3: K15 (16, 17, 18, 19, 20), SM, K16 (17, 18, 19, 20, 21), K wrap tog with wrapped st, K2, M1R, K1, P1, K1, M1L, K5 (4, 3, 2, 1, 0), W&T. 2 sts inc. 114 sts.
Short Row 4: P7 (6, 5, 4, 3, 2), K1, P21 (22, 23, 24, 25, 26), SM, P15 (16, 17, 18, 19, 20), P wrap tog with wrapped st, P2, M1L, P1, K1, P1, M1R, P5 (4, 3, 2, 1, 0), W&T. 2 sts inc. 116 sts.
Short Row 5: K7 (6, 5, 4, 3, 2), P1, K20 (21, 22, 23, 24, 25), SM, K20 (21, 22, 23, 24, 25), M1R, K1, P1, K1, M1L, K6 (5, 4, 3, 2, 1), K wrap tog with wrapped st, K5 (4, 3, 2, 1, 0), M1R, K1, P1, K3, W&T. 3 sts inc. 119 sts.
Short Row 6: P3, K1, P16 (14, 12, 10, 8, 6), K1, P22 (23, 24, 25, 26, 27), SM, P19 (20, 21, 22, 23, 24), M1L, P1, K1, P1, M1R, P6 (5, 4, 3, 2, 1), P wrap tog with wrapped st, P5 (4, 3, 2, 1, 0), M1L, P1, K1, P3, W&T. 3 sts inc. 122 sts.
Short Row 7: K3, P1, K16 (14, 12, 10, 8, 6), P1, K21 (22, 23, 24, 25, 26), SM. 43 (45, 47, 49, 51, 53) sts each for front and back, 16 (14, 12, 10, 8, 6) sts each sleeve, 4 sts for PSs.

Raglan Increases
Rnd 1: K to 1 st before PS, M1R, K1, P1, K1, M1L, K to 1 st before PS, M1R, K1, P1, K1, M1L, K2, K wrap tog with wrapped st, K to 4 sts before PS, K wrap tog with wrapped st, K2, M1R, K1, P1, K1, M1L, K to 1 st before PS, M1R, K1, P1, K1, M1L, K to M. 8 sts inc. 45 (47, 49, 51, 53, 55) sts each for front and back, 18 (16, 14, 12, 10, 8) sts each sleeve, 4 sts for PSs. 130 sts.

Rnd 2: (K to PS, P1) 4 times, K to end of rnd.

Rnd 3 (Inc Rnd): (K to 1 st before PS, M1R, K1, P1, K1, M1L) 4 times, K to end of rnd. 8 sts inc. 138 sts.

Rep Rnds 2-3 another 7 (10, 15, 18, 23, 25) times.

Cont working Rnd 2, working Inc Rnd every fourth rnd, 6 (5, 3, 2, 0, 0) times.

Rep Rnd 2 once more. 73 (79, 87, 93, 101, 107) sts each for front and back, 46 (48, 52, 54, 58, 60) sts each sleeve, 4 sts for PSs. 242 (258, 282, 298, 322, 338) sts total.

Divide Body and Sleeve

K38 (41, 45, 48, 52, 55), place next 46 (48, 52, 54, 58, 60) sts to scrap yarn or stitch holder for Sleeve, CO 17 (19, 19, 21, 21, 23), K75 (81, 89, 95, 103, 109), place next 46 (48, 52, 54, 58, 60) sts to scrap yarn or stitch holder, CO 17 (19, 19, 21, 21, 23) sts, K37 (40, 44, 47, 51, 54). 184 (200, 216, 232, 248, 264) sts.

Body

Rnd 1: K46 (50, 54, 58, 62, 66), P1, K91 (99, 107, 115, 123, 131), P1, K45 (49, 53, 57, 61, 65). 184 (200, 216, 232, 248, 264) sts.

Rnd 2: K37 (40, 44, 47, 51, 54), SSK, K7 (8, 8, 9, 9, 10), P1, K7 (8, 8, 9, 9, 10), K2tog, K73 (79, 87, 93, 101, 107), SSK, K7 (8, 8, 9, 9, 10), P1, K7 (8, 8, 9, 9, 10), K2tog, K36 (39, 43, 46, 50, 54). 4 sts dec. 89 (97, 105, 113, 121, 129) sts each for front and back, 2 sts for PSs. 180 (196, 212, 228, 244, 260) sts total.

Rnd 3: K45 (49, 53, 57, 61, 65), P1, K89 (97, 105, 113, 121, 129), P1, K44 (48, 52, 56, 60, 64).

Rep Rnd 3 for 15" from underarm.

Hem Shaping

Short Row 1 (RS): K45 (49, 53, 57, 61, 65), P1, K21 (23, 25, 27, 29, 31), W&T.

Short Row 2 (WS): P21 (23, 25, 27, 29, 31), K1, P89 (97, 105, 113, 121, 129), K1, P21 (23, 25, 27, 29, 31), W&T.

Short Row 3: K21 (23, 25, 27, 29, 31), P1, K89 (97, 105, 113, 121, 129), P1, K14 (15, 17, 18, 20, 21), W&T.

Short Row 4: P14 (15, 17, 18, 20, 21), K1, P89 (97, 105, 113, 121, 129), K1, P14 (15, 17, 18, 20, 21), W&T.

Short Row 5: K14 (15, 17, 18, 20, 21), P1, K89 (97, 105, 113, 121, 129), P1, K7 (7, 9, 9, 11, 11), W&T.

Short Row 6: P7 (7, 9, 9, 11, 11), K1, P89 (97, 105, 113, 121, 129), K1, P7 (7, 9, 9, 11, 11), W&T.

Short Row 7: K7 (7, 9, 9, 11, 11), P1, K81 (89, 95, 103, 109, 117), W&T.

Short Row 8: P73 (81, 85, 93, 97, 105), W&T.

Short Row 9: K66 (73, 77, 84, 88, 95), W&T.

Short Row 10: P59 (65, 69, 75, 79, 85), W&T.

Short Row 11: K52, (57, 61, 66, 70, 75) W&T.

Short Row 12: P45 (49, 53, 57, 61, 65), W&T.

Short Row 13: K22 (24, 26, 28, 30, 32), SM.

Hem

Setup Rnd: Work in pattern and K wraps tog with wrapped sts at the same time.

Work in pattern around once more, and then switch to smaller needle.

Work 1x1 Rib for 4 rnds.

K all for 3 rnds.

Remove M and BO loosely using larger needle.

Sleeves (make 2 the same)

Place 46 (48, 52, 54, 58, 60) sts from stitch holder onto larger needle, join the new yarn, PU and K 9 (10, 10, 11, 11, 12) sts from center of underarm, K46 (48, 52, 54, 58, 60), PU and K 8 (9, 9, 10, 10, 11) sts, P first picked up st, PM. 63 (67, 71, 75, 79, 83) sts.

Rnd 1: K7 (8, 8, 9, 9, 10), K2tog, K44 (46, 50, 52, 56, 58), SSK, K7 (8, 8, 9, 9, 10), P1. 61 (65, 69, 73, 77, 81) sts.

Rnd 2: K to last st, P1.

Rep Rnd 2 for 12 (12, 10, 10, 8, 8) rnds.

Dec Rnd: K1, K2tog, K to 4 sts before M, SSK, K1, P1. 2 sts dec.

Cont repeating Rnd 2, and Rep Dec Rnd every 12 (10, 9, 8, 8, 7) rnds 7 (8, 9, 10, 11, 12) times. 45 (47, 49, 51, 53, 55) sts.

Cont in pattern until piece measures 17" from underarm, or 1" shorter than desired length.

Switch to smaller needle.

Next Rnd: KFB, work 1x1 Rib to end. 1 st inc.

Work 1x1 Rib for 3 rnds.

K all for 3 rnds.

BO loosely using larger needle.

Finishing

Weave in ends. Block lightly on WS to schematic measurements.

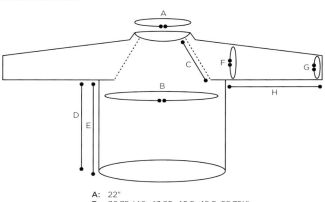

A: 22"
B: 36.75 (40, 43.25, 46.5, 49.5, 52.75)"
C: 9 (9.25, 9.5, 9.75, 10, 10.75)"
D: Front: 16"
E: Back: 18.25"
F: 12.25 (13, 13.75, 14.5, 15.5, 16.25)"
G: 9 (9.25, 9.75, 10, 10.5, 11)"
H: 18"

...to stay in.

COZY COUCH SOCKS

by Kathy Lewinski

FINISHED MEASUREMENTS
7 (8, 9, 10)" finished foot circumference
at widest point; 8.5 (9.5, 10.5, 11.5)"
finished length from toe to heel

YARN
Knit Picks Andean Treasure (sport
weight, 100% Baby Alpaca; 110 yards/
50g): MC Fog Heather 23490, 3 balls;
C1 Prairie Heather 24938, 1 ball

NEEDLES
US 2 (2.75mm) DPNs, or size
to obtain gauge

NOTIONS
Yarn Needle
Stitch Marker
Scrap Yarn

GAUGE
32 sts and 40 rows = 4" in stockinette
stitch in the round, blocked

Cozy Couch Socks

Notes:

These slipper socks are just the thing for a lazy day on the couch with a good book and a cup of cocoa. Knit in baby alpaca, they are slouchy, soft, and oh, so cozy. These socks are worked from the top down with an afterthought heel. The foot of the sock can easily be lengthened or shortened by changing the amount that is worked between the heel and toe.

1x1 Rib (in the rnd over a multiple of 2 sts)
All Rnds: (K1, P1) to end.

Kitchener Stitch

A tutorial for the Kitchener Stitch can be found at https://tutorials.knitpicks.com/kitchener-stitch/.

DIRECTIONS

Cuff

Loosely CO 56 (64, 72, 80) sts with MC. Divide between three needles. Join tog to work in the rnd being careful not to twist sts, PM between the first and last st to mark rnds. Work in 1x1 Rib for 1".

Leg

K every rnd for 8".

Place Yarn for Heel

K28 (32, 36, 40) sts with scrap yarn. Move those 28 (32, 36, 40) sts back onto the left needle.

Foot

K every rnd for 5 (5.5, 6, 6.25)" or until about 3.5 (4, 4.5, 5.25)" shorter than desired sock length.

Toe

Switch to C1.

Rnd 1: K1, SSK, K22 (26, 30, 34), K2tog, K2, SSK, K22 (26, 30, 34), K2tog, K1. 4 sts dec.

Rnd 2: K all.

Rep Rnds 1 and 2 until 28 (32, 36, 40) sts remain.

Rep Rnd 1 until 16 sts remain.

Put the first 8 sts on one needle and the second 8 sts on a second needle.

Graft using Kitchener Stitch.

Heel

PU the 28 (32, 36, 40) sts below and the 28 (32, 36, 40) sts above the scrap yarn. Carefully remove the scrap yarn. Divide the 56 (64, 72, 80) sts between 3 needles to work in the rnd. PM on the right side between the upper and lower sts to mark rnd.

Work as for Toe; to avoid a gap between the upper and lower sts of the heel, PU a st from the foot of the sock and knit it tog with the st before it the first time you work Rnd 1.

Finishing

Weave in ends and block.

EMBERLY CARDIGAN

by Jen Dwyer

FINISHED MEASUREMENTS

38.5 (42, 46, 50, 54, 58)" finished bust
measurement; garment is meant to be
worn with 6-8" of positive ease

YARN

Knit Picks Wonderfluff (bulky weight,
70% Baby Alpaca, 7% Merino Wool,
23% Nylon; 142 yards/50g): Cobblestone
Heather 27187, 8 (9, 9, 10, 11 12) balls

NEEDLES

US 10.5 (6.5mm) straight and 16" circular
needles, plus 32" and 48" circular
needles, or size to obtain gauge

NOTIONS

Yarn Needle
Stitch Markers

GAUGE

16 sts and 27 rows = 4" in garter stitch,
blocked

Emberly Cardigan

Notes:

The Emberly Cardigan is perfect for snuggling up with a cup of tea before the fire on a cold winter evening. Generously sized, the sweater envelops you in warmth while still being lightweight and easy to wear. Designed with the beginning knitter in mind, this cardigan is worked entirely in garter and rib stitches. Each piece of the sweater is worked flat and seamed as you go. The diagonal front panels are created with simple decreases and decorated with useful pockets. Such a cozy yet beautiful sweater is sure to be the one you grab again and again all winter long.

Garter Stitch (worked flat over any number of sts)
All Rows: Knit.

1x1 Rib (worked flat over an even number of sts)
All Rows: (K1, P1) to end.

DIRECTIONS

Left Front Panel
Work front panels with straight or circular needles.
CO 38 (42, 46, 50, 54, 58) sts.
Work 1x1 Rib for 15 rows.
K all for 2 (0, 4, 2, 4, 2) rows.

First Decrease
Mark RS facing you with stitch marker.
Row 1 (RS): K1, SSK, K across. 1 st dec.
Rows 2-10: K across.
Rep Rows 1-10 12 (10, 10, 4, 4, 5) more times. 25 (31, 35, 45, 49, 52) sts.

Second Decrease
Row 1 (RS): K1, SSK, K across. 1 st dec.
Rows 2-8: K across.
Rep Rows 1-8 2 (5, 5, 13, 13, 12) more times. 22 (25, 29, 31, 35, 39) sts.
BO.

Right Front Panel
Rep Left Front Panel, until First Decrease.

First Decrease
Mark RS facing you with stitch marker.
Row 1 (RS): K across until 3 sts remain, K2tog, K1. 1 st dec.
Rows 2-10: K across.
Rep Rows 1-10 12 (10, 10, 4, 4, 5) more times. 25 (31, 35, 45, 49, 52) sts.

Second Decrease
Row 1 (RS): K across until 3 sts remain, K2tog, K1. 1 st dec.
Rows 2-8: K across.
Rep rows 1-8 2 (5, 5, 13, 13, 12) more times. 22 (25, 29, 31, 35, 39) sts.
BO and weave in loose ends.
Block both front panels to finished dimensions.

Back Panel

Work back panel with 32" circular needles. CO 76 (84, 92, 100, 108, 116) sts.
Work 1x1 Rib for 15 Rows.
K all for 156 (158, 162, 164, 166, 166) rows.
BO and weave in loose ends.
Block back panel to finished dimensions.

To join front panels to back panel at the shoulder seam, begin by placing front panels face down on top of back panel, ensuring that the long straight edges of the front panels line up with the sides of the back panel. The diagonal edges are towards the center and they may not touch at the bottom ribbing. Begin at the top outer corners of the panels with yarn and yarn needle. Sew each shoulder seam with a whip stitch or your preferred method. Weave in loose ends.

Front Ribbing

With 48" circular needles, begin at the front bottom corner and PU sts along the diagonal edge of the first front panel, the back neck edge and diagonal edge of the second front panel, ending at the other bottom front corner.
PU approximately one st for every other row on the front panels, and one st for each st along the back neck.
Ensure that you have an even number of sts.
Work 1x1 Rib for 3 rows.
BO in pattern. Block ribbing gently if desired.

Sleeves (make 2 the same)

Work sleeves with straight or circular needles. CO 52 (54, 56, 60, 66, 74) sts.
K all for 7 rows.

First Decrease

Dec Row (RS): K1, SSK, K across until 3 sts remain, K2tog, K1.
2 sts dec.
K all for 9 (11, 9, 7, 5, 5) rows.
Beginning again with Dec Row, rep these 10 (12, 10, 8, 6, 6) rows 1 (7, 5, 5, 2, 16) more times. 48 (38, 44, 48, 60, 40) sts.
Sizes 42 and 58 are finished decreasing. Skip down to cuff instructions.

Second Decrease
Sizes 38.5, 46, 50, and 54" Only
Dec Row (RS): K1, SSK, K across until 3 sts remain, K2tog, K1.
2 sts dec.
Knit 11 (0, 11, 9, 7, 0) rows.
Beginning again with Dec Row 1, rep these 12 (0, 12, 10, 8, 0) rows 5 (0, 2, 4, 9, 0) more times. 36 (38, 38, 38, 40, 40) sts.

Cuff

Work 1x1 Rib for 15 rows.
BO in pattern and weave in loose ends.
Block both sleeves to finished dimensions.

To join sleeve to sweater, lay sweater flat (separating the front and back) with RS facing up. Find the midpoint of the top edge of the sleeve. Lay the sleeve face down on top of the sweater, matching the midpoint of the sleeve to the shoulder seam at the outer edge of the sweater. The cuff of the sleeve should be pointing towards the neck opening. See diagram for attaching the sleeve. Beginning at the midpoint, whip stitch the top edge of the sleeve to the sweater. Begin again at the midpoint and rep for the other side. Weave in loose ends. Rep for the other sleeve.

Side Seams

To join the side seams, begin by folding the sleeve and the sweater RSs together, matching the armpits at the seam. Beginning at the armpit, sew the sleeve together, ending at the cuff. Begin again at the armpit and sew the side seam of the sweater. It may be helpful to use clips to hold the sides together evenly as you sew.
Rep for the other side.

Pockets (make 2 the same)

Work pockets with straight or 16" circular needles.
CO 16 sts, leaving a long tail for sewing pocket on.
Work in 1x1 Rib for 7 rows.
K all for 20 rows.
BO, leaving a long tail. Weave in loose ends except for long tail. Block to 4" square.
Center each pocket on a front panel about 2" above the ribbing. Use the long tail and yarn needle to sew each pocket to the front panel on three sides, leaving the top open.

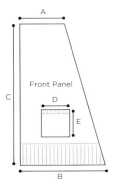

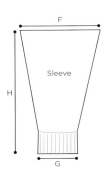

A: 5.5 (6.25, 7.25, 7.75, 8.85, 9.75)"
B: 9.5 (10.5, 11.5, 12.5, 13.5, 14.5)"
C: 25.25 (25.5, 26.25, 26.5, 26.75, 26.75)"
D: 4"
E: 4"
F: 13 (13.5, 14, 15, 16.5, 18.5)"
G: 9 (9.5, 9.5, 9.5, 10, 10)"
H: 10.75 (11.25, 12, 13, 14.5, 16.5)"
I: 19 (21, 23, 25, 27, 29)"
J: 25.25 (25.5, 26.25, 26.5, 26.75, 26.75)"

Attaching Sleeves

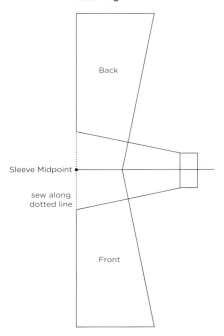

GWYN

by Maria Leigh

FINISHED MEASUREMENT

37.25 (40.5, 43.75, 47, 50, 53.25)" finished bust measurement

YARN

Knit Picks Stroll (fingering weight, 75% Fine Superwash Merino Wool, 25% Nylon; 231 yards/50g): Dogwood Heather 25603, 4 (4, 5, 5, 6, 6) skeins; White 26082, 2 (2, 2, 3, 3, 3) skeins
Knit Picks Aloft (lace weight, 72% Super Kid Mohair, 28% Silk; 260 yards/25g): Blush 25205, 4 (4, 5, 5, 6, 6) balls; White 25213, 2 (2, 2, 3, 3, 3) balls

NEEDLES

US 8 (5mm) 32" and 16" circular needles, or size to obtain gauge

US 7 (4.5mm) 40" circular needle, or one size smaller than size used to obtain gauge

NOTIONS

Yarn Needle
Stitch Markers
Moveable Stitch Marker or
Small Safety Pin
Stitch Holders or Scrap Yarn

GAUGE

20 sts and 26 rows = 4" in stockinette stitch with yarns held together on larger needles, lightly blocked

Gwyn

Notes:

Gwyn is a top-down cozy cardigan sweater worked by holding together Stroll Fingering and Aloft yarns. It features a unique set-in sleeve construction with no seaming, and a curved V-neck line gives a very feminine look.

C1: 1 strand each of Stroll Sock Dogwood Heather and Aloft Blush, held together.
C2: 1 strand each of Stroll Sock White and Aloft White, held together.

Stockinette Stitch (worked flat over any number of sts)
Row 1: Knit.
Row 2: Purl.
Rep Rows 1-2 for pattern.

2x2 Rib (worked flat over multiples of four sts)
All Rows: (K2, P2) to end.

Wrap and Turn (W&T)
A tutorial for the Wrap and Turn (W&T) can be found at http://tutorials.knitpicks.com/wptutorials/short-rows-wrap-and-turn-or-wt/.

DIRECTIONS
Body
Back Shoulder
Using C1, CO 76 (78, 80, 82, 84, 86) sts with larger needle.
Setup Row (WS): P13 (14, 15, 16, 17, 18), PM, P50, PM, P13 (14, 15, 16, 17, 18).
Row 1 (RS): K to M, SM, K5, SSK, K to 7 sts before M, K2tog, K5, SM, K to end. 2 sts dec.
Rows 2, 4: P across.
Row 3: K to M, SM, K4, SSK, K to 6 sts before M, K2tog, K4, SM, K to end. 2 sts dec.
Row 5: K to M, SM, K3, SSK, K to 5 sts before M, K2tog, K3, SM, K to end. 2 sts dec. 70 (72, 74, 76, 78, 80) sts.
Row 6 (WS): P across, removing Ms.
Break yarn.
Turn garment so RS is facing.

Right Front Shoulder
Rotate garment clockwise 180 degrees, PU 13 (14, 15, 16, 17, 18) sts on the end of Back Shoulder CO edge.
Setup Row (WS): P across.
Row 1 (RS): K8 (9, 10, 10, 11, 12), W&T.
Rows 2, 4: P across.
Row 3: K3 (4, 4, 5, 5, 5), W&T.
Row 5: K3 (4, 4, 5, 5, 5), K wrap tog with wrapped st, K4 (4, 5, 4, 5, 6), K wrap tog with wrapped st, K3 (4, 4, 5, 5, 5).
Row 6 (WS): Purl across.
Break yarn. 13 (14, 15, 16, 17, 18) sts.

Left Front Shoulder
With RS facing, PU and K 13 (14, 15, 16, 17, 18) sts on the start of Back Shoulder CO edge.
Setup Row (WS): P across.
Row 1 (RS): K3 (4, 4, 5, 5, 5), W&T.

Rows 2, 4: P across.
Row 3: K3 (4, 4, 5, 5, 5), K wrap tog with wrapped st, K4 (4, 5, 4, 5, 6), W&T.
Row 5: 8 (9, 10, 10, 11, 12), K wrap tog with wrapped st, K3 (4, 4, 5, 5, 5).
Row 6 (WS): Purl across.
Do not break yarn. Turn garment so RS is facing to prepare to work Yoke. 13 (14, 15, 16, 17, 18) sts on each front and 70 (72, 74, 76, 78, 80) sts on back.

Yoke
Sts are increased at each front neck, each side of the sleeve caps, and the armholes on the body in the Yoke section. The Yoke is divided by markers for Left Front, Left Sleeve, Back, Right Sleeve, and Right Front.
Row 1 (RS): K2, M1L, K11 (12, 13, 14, 15, 16), PM, PU and K 10 sts on the shoulder edge for Left Sleeve Cap, PM, K70 (72, 74, 76, 78, 80), PM, PU and K 10 sts on the shoulder edge for Right Sleeve Cap, PM, K11 (12, 13, 14, 15, 16), M1R, K2. 118 (122, 126, 130, 134, 138) sts.
Row 2 and all WS rows: Purl across.
Please follow the Yoke Table from Row 3 to Row 43 (45, 47, 49, 51, 53), utilizing the increases listed below.
Neck Only Inc Row (RS): K2, M1L, K to last 2 sts, M1R, K2. 2 sts inc.
Sleeve Cap Only Increase Row (RS): (Work in pattern to M, SM, M1L, K to next M, M1R, SM) twice, cont in pattern to end of Row. 4 sts inc.
Neck and Sleeve Cap Only Inc Row (RS): K2, M1L, (K to M, SM, M1L, K to M, M1R, SM) twice, K to last 2 sts, M1R, K2. 6 sts inc.
Neck, Sleeve Cap and Armhole Increases, beginning at Row 37 (RS): K2, M1L, (K to 1 st before M, M1R, K1, SM, M1L, K to next M, M1R, SM, K1, M1L) twice, K to last 2 sts, M1R, K2. 10 sts inc.
End with WS Row 44 (46, 48, 50, 52, 54). 36 (38, 40, 42, 44, 46) sts for each front, 52 sts for each sleeve, and 78 (82, 86, 90, 94, 98) sts for back. 254 (262, 270, 278, 286, 294) sts total.

Divide Sleeves and Body
Next Row (RS): K2, M1L, K to M, SM, place next 52 sts to scrap yarn for Left Sleeve, CO 13 (17, 21, 25, 29, 33) sts for left underarm, SM, K to M, SM, place next 52 sts to scrap yarn for Right Sleeve, CO 13 (17, 21, 25, 29, 33) sts for right underarm, SM, K to 2 sts before end, M1R, K2. 178 (194, 210, 226, 242, 258) sts.

Main Body
Next Row (WS): P across.
Row 1 (RS): (K to 1 st before M, remove M, SSK, K5 (7, 9, 11, 13, 15), PM, P1, PM, K5 (7, 9, 11, 13, 15), remove M, K2tog) twice, K to end. 42 (46, 50, 54, 58, 62) sts for each Front, 88 (96, 104, 112, 120, 128) sts for Back, 2 P sts for side seam. 174 (190, 206, 222, 238, 254) sts.

Row 2 and all WS rows: Purl across.

Row 3 and all RS rows: (K to M, SM, p1, SM) twice, K to end.
Rep Rows 2-3 for 23 rows or 4" from underarm. End with a WS row.

Inc Row (RS): (K to 1 st before M, M1R, K1, SM, P1, SM, K1, M1L) twice, K to end. 4 sts inc.
Cont in pattern, repeating Inc Row every 26 rows, or every 4", twice more. 186 (202, 218, 234, 250, 266) sts.
Cont in pattern until piece measures 15" from Underarm CO edge. End with a WS row.

Body Bottom

Break C1 and switch to C2.

Next Row (RS): K12 (14, 16, 18, 20, 22), place next 28 sts on stitch holder, CO 30 sts, cont in pattern to last M, SM, K6 (7, 9, 11, 13, 15), place next 28 sts on stitch holder, CO 30 sts, cont in pattern to end.

Next Row (WS): P11 (13, 15, 17, 19, 21). SSP, P28, P2tog, P to last M, SM, P5 (6, 8, 10, 12, 14), SSP, P28, P2tog, P to end.
Cont in pattern next 4 rows. End with a WS row.
Rep Inc Row once.
Cont in pattern until piece measures 20" from Underarm CO edge. 190 (206, 222, 238, 254, 270) sts.
Rep Inc Row once more.
Cont in pattern 1" more, for a total of 21" from Underarm CO edge. End with a WS row. 194 (210, 226, 242, 258, 274) sts.
Hold remaining sts while making Pockets.

Pocket (make 2 the same)

With RS facing, remove 28 sts from holder to larger needle. Using C2, work flat in St st across the 28 sts for 6", ending with a WS row. Break yarn.

Join Pockets: Return to body sts, K12 (14, 16, 18, 20, 22) sts, then K tog 1 body st with 1 Left Inner Pocket st until all 28 pocket sts have been joined. Cont in pattern to last 40 (42, 44, 46, 48, 50) sts, K tog next 28 Body sts with Right Inner Pocket as done for the Left Pocket, K to end.
Cont in pattern until piece measures 23" from Underarm CO edge, ending with a WS row.
BO all sts loosely and remove Ms.

Sleeves (make 2 the same)

Remove 52 sts from the scrap yarn to larger needle.
Using C1, PU and K 7 (9, 11, 13, 15, 17) sts from center of underarm, K52, PU and K 6 (8, 10, 12, 14, 16) sts to center of underarm, PM, P first picked up st, PM. 65 (69, 73, 77, 81, 85) sts.

Setup Rnd: K5 (7, 9, 11, 13, 15), K2tog, K50, SSK, K5 (7, 9, 11, 13, 15), SM, P1, SM. 63 (67, 71, 75, 79, 83) sts.
Cont in pattern for 3.5" from PU edge.

Dec Rnd: K1, K2tog, K to 3 sts before M, SSK, K1, SM, P1, SM. 2 sts dec.
Cont in pattern, repeating Dec Rnd every 20 (18, 16, 14, 12, 10) rnds 3 (4, 5, 6, 7, 8) more times. 55 (57, 59, 61, 63, 65) sts.
Cont to WE as established, and AT THE SAME TIME, break C1 and switch to C2 at 15" from PU edge.
Cont in pattern until sleeve measures 21" from PU edge or desired sleeve length. BO all sts loosely and remove Ms.

Neck Band

With C2 and smaller needle, PU and K 112 sts along the right front opening, PU and K 31 (33, 35, 37, 39, 41) sts along the right front neck, PU and K 50 sts on the back neck, PU and K 31 (33, 35, 37, 39, 41) sts along left front neck, PU and K 112 sts along the left front opening. 336 (340, 344, 348, 352, 356) sts.

Next Row (WS): P3, work 2x2 Rib to last st, P1.
Cont in 2X2 Rib until band measures 1.25" ending with a WS row.
BO all sts loosely.

Finishing

Whip stitch the Inner Pocket seam along purl ridge on Body on WS.

Weave in ends. Block lightly on WS to schematic measurements.

Yoke Table

N: Neckline   SC: Sleeve Cap   AH: Armhole   ●: Increase

Size	37.25"			40.5"			43.75"			47"			50"			53.25"		
Row (RS)	N	SC	AH	N	SC	AH	N	SC	AH	N	SC	AH	N	SC	AH	N	SC	AH
Row 3		●			●		●				●		●				●	
Row 5	●	●		●	●			●		●	●		●	●		●	●	
Row 7		●			●		●				●		●				●	
Row 9	●	●		●	●			●		●	●		●	●		●	●	
Row 11		●			●		●				●			●			●	
Row 13	●	●		●	●			●		●	●			●		●	●	
Row 15	●	●			●		●			●	●			●		●	●	
Row 17	●	●		●	●			●		●	●			●		●	●	
Row 19	●	●		●	●		●				●			●		●		
Row 21		●			●		●	●			●		●			●	●	
Row 23	●	●			●		●	●			●		●			●	●	
Row 25	●	●		●	●			●		●	●					●	●	
Row 27	●	●			●		●	●		●	●					●	●	
Row 29	●	●		●	●			●		●	●		●			●	●	
Row 31	●	●		●	●		●	●		●	●		●	●		●	●	
Row 33	●	●		●	●		●	●		●	●					●	●	
Row 35	●	●		●	●		●	●		●	●		●			●		
Row 37	●	●	●	●	●	●	●	●	●	●	●	●	●	●	●	●	●	●
Row 39	●	●	●	●	●	●	●	●	●	●	●	●	●	●	●	●	●	●
Row 41	●	●	●	●	●	●	●	●	●	●	●	●	●	●	●	●	●	●
Row 43	●	●	●	●	●	●	●	●	●	●	●	●	●	●	●	●	●	●
Row 45				●	●	●	●	●	●	●	●	●	●	●	●	●	●	●
Row 47							●	●	●	●	●	●	●	●	●	●	●	●
Row 49										●	●	●	●	●	●	●	●	●
Row 51													●	●	●	●	●	●
Row 53																●	●	●

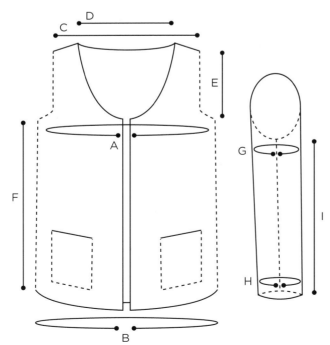

A: 37.25 (40.5, 43.75, 47, 50, 53.25)"
B: 41.25 (44.5, 47.75, 51, 54, 57.25)"
C: 14 (14.5, 14.75, 15.25, 15.5, 16)"
D: 10"
E: 7 (7.25, 7.75, 8, 8.25, 8.5)"
F: 23"
G: 12.5 (13.5, 14.25, 15, 15.75, 16.5)"
H: 11 (11.5, 11.75, 12.25, 12.5, 13)"
I: 21"

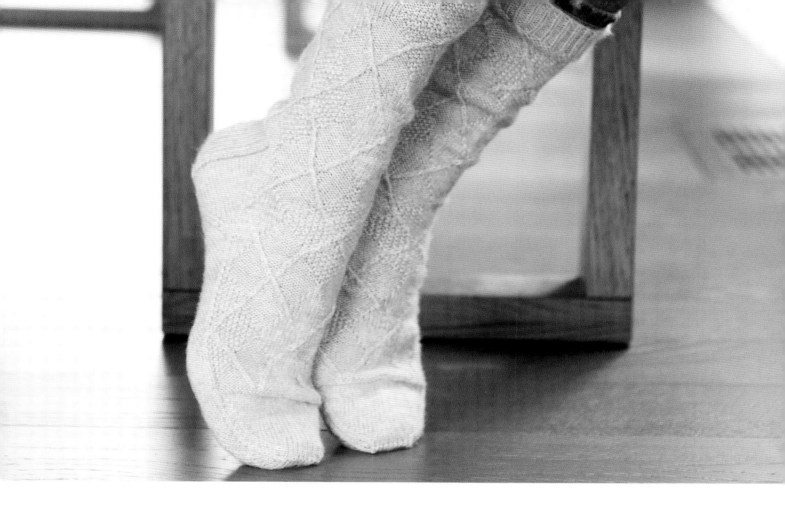

HOT TODDY SOCKS

by Meredith Wills

FINISHED MEASUREMENTS

7.5 (8, 8.5, 9, 9.5, 10, 10.5)″ foot and
7.5 (8.5, 8.5, 9.25, 10, 10, 11)″ leg
circumference; socks are meant to be
worn with zero or slight negative ease

YARN

Knit Picks Stroll (fingering weight, 75%
Fine Superwash Merino Wool, 25% Nylon;
231 yards/50g): Dogwood Heather
25603; 2 (2, 3, 3, 3, 4, 4) skeins

NEEDLES

US 1 (2.25mm) DPNs or two 24″ circular
needles for two circulars technique, or
one 32″ or longer circular needle for
Magic Loop technique, or size to obtain
gauge

NOTIONS

Yarn Needle
Stitch Markers
Small Cable Needle
Scrap Yarn or Stitch Holder

GAUGE

38 sts and 50 rows = 4″ in stockinette
stitch in the round, blocked
38 sts and 54 rows = 4″ in Main Chart
Pattern in the round, blocked

Hot Toddy Socks

Notes:

What better way to enjoy a strong, warming drink by the fire than in these comfy, argyle-inspired Hot Toddy Socks! This top-down pattern uses texture, rather than color, to create an argyle look, relying only on stockinette, reverse stockinette, seed stitch, and single-stitch cables, while the worked-in arch support makes them extra snuggly.

With seven available sizes, this pattern is tailored for both women and men. These Hot Toddies are the kind of socks you'll want to show off, rather than wearing them with shoes—perfect for keeping your feet warm on a cold night.

When working charts in the rnd, read all chart rows from right to left, as RS rows.

Kitchener Stitch
A tutorial for the Kitchener Stitch can be found at https://tutorials.knitpicks.com/kitchener-stitch/.

1x1 Rib (in the rnd over an even number of sts)
All Rnds: *P1, K1; rep from * to end of rnd.

Special Main Chart Sts
Red/Purple Squares: Work previous rnd to one st before end of rnd (red squares). Work "cross 1 over 1 left/purl bg" cable using last st of previous rnd and first two sts of new rnd. Work two reps of Main Chart to one st before end of rnd. Work last st as K1 TBL (purple square).
Green/Blue Squares: Work first st of Rnd 19 (21, 21, 23, 25, 25, 27) as P1 (green square). Work two reps of Main Chart to end of rnd. Work first st of Rnd 20 (22, 22, 24, 26, 26, 28) as K1 (blue square). Cont as established.

Special Instep Chart Sts
Orange Squares: For Rnds 20 (22, 22, 24, 26, 26, 28) and 58 (64, 64, 70, 76, 76, 82), work st before Instep Chart and st after Instep Chart together with Instep Chart sts as part of a "cross 1 over 1 right/purl bg" cable (orange squares).

DIRECTIONS
The sock is worked in the rnd, starting from the top down.

Cuff
Loosely CO 72 (80, 80, 88, 96, 96, 104) sts. Join in the rnd. PM to mark beginning of rnd, being careful not to twist sts. Work 1x1 Rib for 15 (15, 15, 15, 18, 18, 18) rnds, ending 1 st before end of final rnd.

Leg
The leg is worked using the Main Charts. Rep Main Chart for your size twice across for each rnd.
Leg Setup Rnd: Starting with last st of final Cuff rnd, follow instructions for "Red/Purple Squares" to work first rnd of Main Chart.
Work Main Chart for your size to end.

Heel
The heel is worked flat, using short rows for the Heel Turn.
Heel Setup: P1, K1 TBL, P7 (8, 8, 9, 10, 10, 13), place next 37 (41, 41, 45, 49, 49, 53) sts on stitch holder. Turn. P35 (39, 39, 43, 47, 47, 51) heel sts. Turn.

Heel Flap
Heel Flap Stitch
Row 1 (RS): *SL1, K1; rep from * to 1 st from end, K1.
Row 2 (WS): SL1, P to end.
Work 18 (19, 20, 21, 22, 23, 24) reps of Heel Flap St Rows.

Heel Turn
Short Row 1 (RS): SL1, K19 (21, 21, 25, 27, 27, 29), SSK, K1. Turn. 1 st dec.
Short Row 2 (WS): SL1, P4 (6, 6, 8, 8, 8, 8), P2tog, P1. Turn. 1 st dec.
Short Rows 1 and 2 will create a "gap" after each slipped st.
Short Row 3: SL1, K to 1 st before gap, Ssk across gap, K1. Turn. 1 st dec.
Short Row 4: SL1, P to 1 st before gap, P2tog across gap, P1. Turn. 1 st dec.
Rep Short Rows 3 and 4 until all Heel Flap sts have been worked. 19 (23, 23, 25, 27, 27, 29) heel sts.

Gusset
The gusset is worked in the rnd, using the Instep Charts, and includes arch shaping.
Gusset Setup Rnd 1: K19 (23, 23, 25, 27, 27, 29), PU and K 19 (20, 21, 22, 23, 24, 25) sts from edge of heel flap, work Row 1 of Instep Chart for your size, PU and K TBL 19 (20, 21, 22, 23, 24, 25) sts from edge of heel flap, K9 (11, 11, 12, 13, 13, 14), PM to mark new beginning of rnd. 94 (104, 106, 114, 122, 124, 132) sts.
Gusset Setup Rnd 2: K3, PM, K to Instep Chart, work Row 2 of Instep Chart, K to 2 sts before end of rnd, PM, K to end.

Gusset/Arch Creation Rnd 1: K2, M1L, K to M, SM, SSK, K to 2 sts before Instep Chart, K2tog, work Instep Chart, SSK, K to 2 sts before M, K2tog, SM, K to 1 st before end of rnd, M1R, K to end. 2 sts dec.
Gusset/Arch Creation Rnd 2: Work as established.

FOR ALL SIZES EXCEPT 8": Rep Gusset/Arch Creation Rnds 1 and 2 until 70 (--, 80, 86, 90, 96, 100) sts remain. 24 (--, 26, 28, 32, 28, 32) sts dec. Continue with Arch Creation Rnds 1 and 2 (below) until 2 sts remain between Ms and Instep Chart, then work Arch Creation Finishing Rnd.

Arch Creation Rnd 1: K2, M1L, K to M, SM, SSK, K to Instep Chart, work Instep Chart, K to 2 sts before M, K2tog, SM, K to 1 st before end of rnd, M1R, K to end.
Arch Creation Rnd 2: Work as established.

Arch Creation Finishing Rnd: K2, M1L, K to M, remove M, K2tog, work Instep Chart, SSK, remove M, K to 1 st before end of rnd, M1R, K to end.
Work one rnd as established.

FOR 8″ SIZE ONLY: Rep Gusset/Arch Creation Rnds 1 and 2 until 3 sts remain between Ms and Instep Chart. 26 sts dec, 78 sts remain. Then work Gusset/Arch Creation Finishing Rnd (below).

Gusset/Arch Creation Finishing Rnd, Size 8″ ONLY: K2, M1L, K to M, remove M, SL1 K-wise twice, move sts back to LH needle, K3tog, work Instep Chart, SL1 K-wise, K2tog, PSSO, remove M, K to 1 st before end of rnd, M1R, K to end. 2 sts dec, 76 sts.

Work one rnd as established.

Final count will be 70 (76, 80, 86, 90, 96, 100) foot sts.

Foot

The foot is worked in the rnd, while continuing to use Instep Charts, and includes arch shaping.

Arch Shaping Rnd 1: K2, M1L, K to two sts before Instep Chart, K2tog, work Instep Chart, SSK, K to 1 st before end of rnd, M1R, K to end.

Arch Shaping Rnd 2: Work as established.
Rep Arch Shaping Rnds 1 and 2 1 (3, 1, 2, 5, 1, 4) times, then Arch Shaping Rnd 1 once.

Arch Finishing Setup Rnd: K2, PM, work as established to 1 st before end of rnd, PM, K to end.

Arch Finishing Rnd 1: K to M, M1R, SM, K to 2 sts before Instep Chart, K2tog, work Instep Chart, SSK, K to M, SM, M1L, K to end.

Arch Finishing Rnd 2: Work as established.

Rep Arch Finishing Rnds 1 and 2 until 1 st remains between M and Instep Chart.

Work as established until foot measures 1.75 (2, 2, 2.25, 2.25, 2.5, 2.5)″ shorter than total desired foot length, repeating Instep Chart if necessary.

Toe

The toe is worked in St st and begins with a purled ridge, after which it decreases in the rnd.

Toe Setup Rnds: K to Instep Chart, P37 (41, 41, 45, 49, 49, 53), K to end of rnd. K 18 (19, 20, 22, 23, 24, 25), PM to mark new beginning of rnd. K 35 (38, 40, 43, 45, 48, 50), PM, K to end.

Toe Rnd 1: *K1, SSK, K to 3 (2, 2, 3, 3, 2, 2) sts before M, K2tog, K1 (0, 0, 1, 1, 0, 0); rep from * twice. 4 sts dec.
Toe Rnd 2: K all.
Rep Toe Rnds 1 and 2 until 38 (40, 40, 42, 46, 48, 52) sts remain.
Rep Toe Rnd 1 until 18 (20, 20, 22, 26, 28, 28) sts remain.

Toe Finishing (SIZES 8, 8.5, 10, 10.5″ ONLY): K2tog, K to 1 st before M, SSK. 18 (18, 18, 22, 26, 26, 26) toe sts.

All Sizes: Graft instep and sole together using Kitchener Stitch.

Finishing

Weave in ends, wash, and block lightly.

Main Chart - 7.5 inches

Legend:

☐ **Knit**
Knit stitch

⊡ **Purl**
Purl stitch

■ **No Stitch**
Placeholder - No stitch made

Ⓑ **Knit TBL**
Knit stitch through the back loop

◹◸ **Right Twist**
SL1 to CN, hold in back. K1, K1 from CN

◺◹ **Left Twist**
SL1 to CN, hold in front. K1, K1 from CN

◹◸ **Right Twist, Purl bg**
SL1 to CN, hold in back. K1, P1 from CN

◺◹ **Left Twist, Purl bg**
SL1 to CN, hold in front. P1, K1 from CN

◺◹◸ **Cross 1 Over 1 Right**
SL2 to CN, hold in back. K1, SL center st from CN
back to left hand needle and knit it. K1 from CN

◺◹◸ **Cross 1 Over 1 Left/Purl bg**
SL2 to CN, hold in front. K1, SL center st from CN
back to left hand needle and purl it. K1 from CN

◺◹◸ **Cross 1 Over 1 Right/Purl bg**
SL2 to CN, hold in back. K1, SL center st from CN
back to left hand needle and purl it. K1 from CN

☐ **Red Square**
Work cable over last st of previous rnd and
2 st of current rnd

☐ **Orange Square**
Work st before chart and st after chart as cable

☐ **Purple Square**
Work last st of rnd K1 TBL

☐ **Green Square**
Work first st of rnd as P1

☐ **Blue Square**
Work first st of rnd as K1

Instep Chart - 7.5 inches

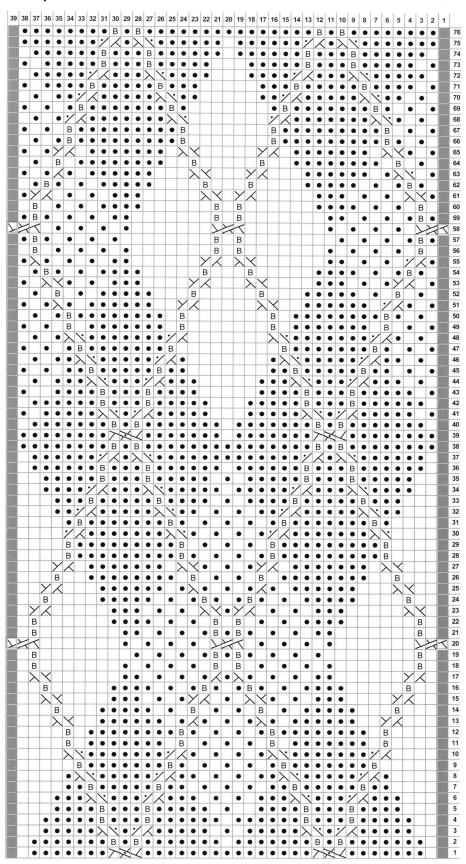

Main Chart - 8, 8.5 inches

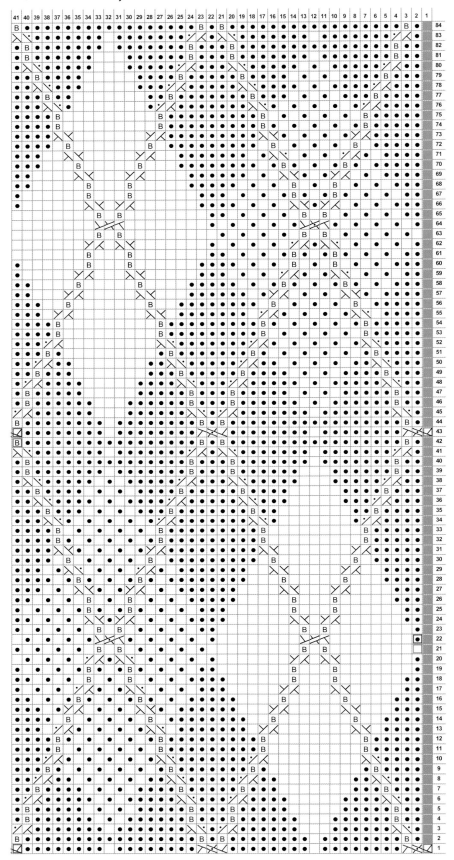

Instep Chart - 8, 8.5 inches

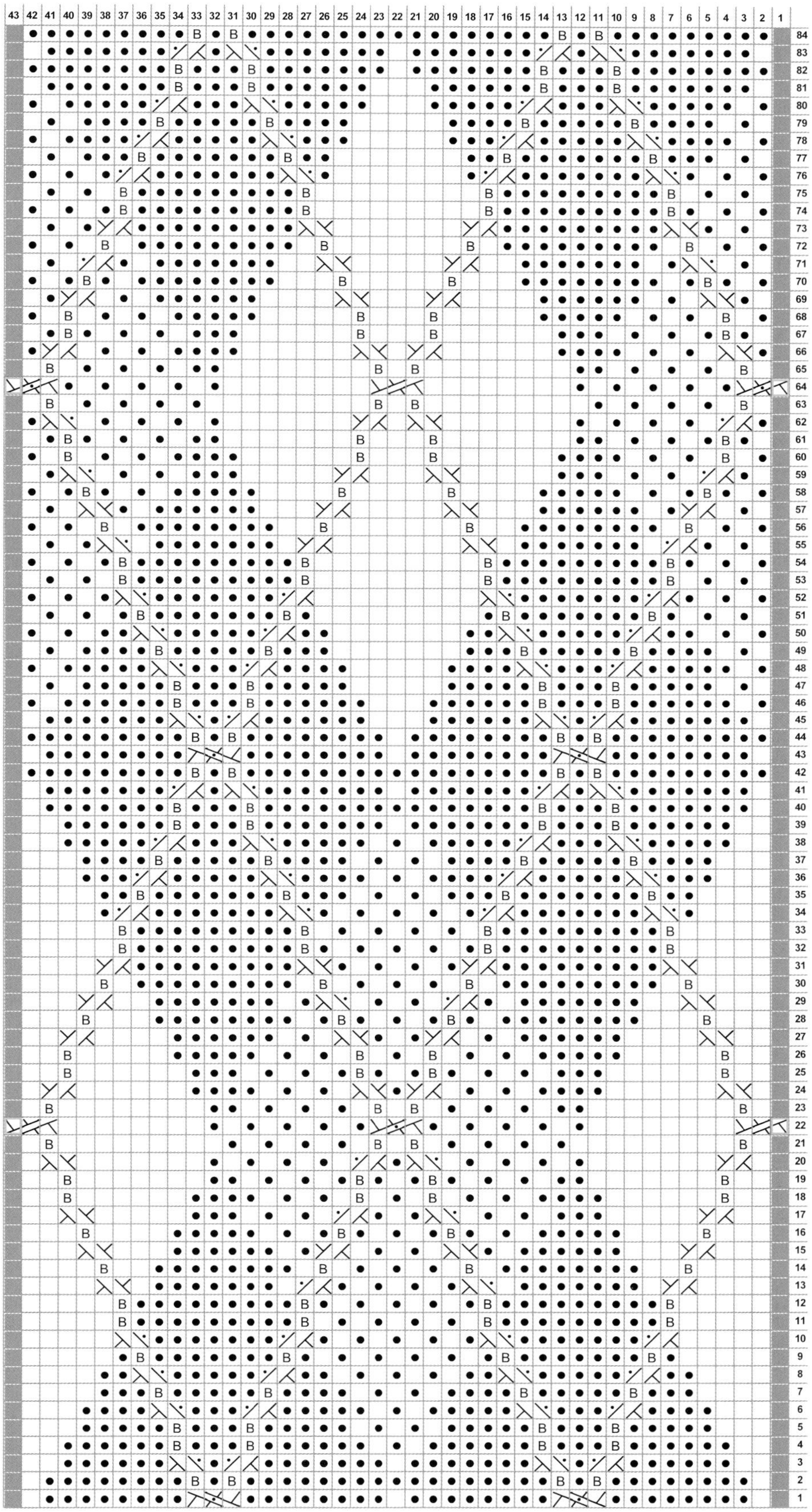

Main Chart - 9 inches

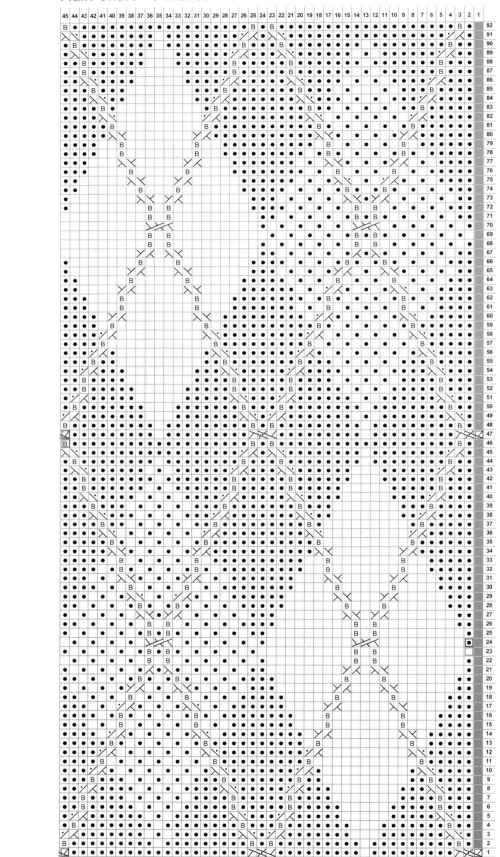

Instep Chart - 9 inches

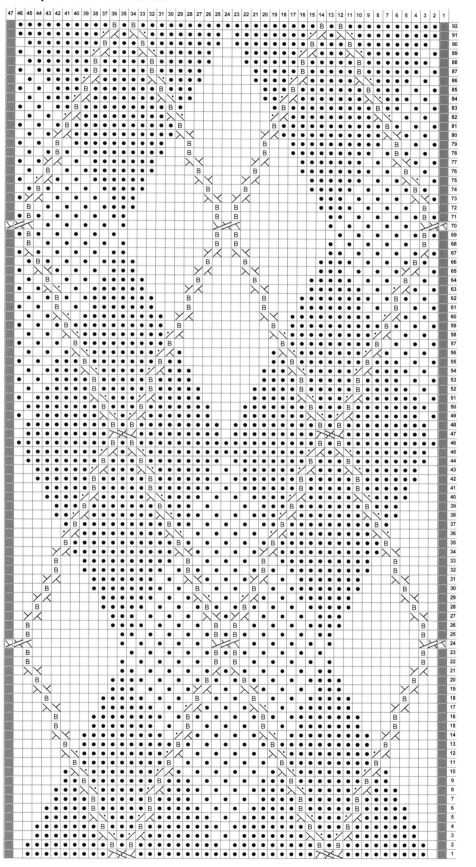

Main Chart - 9.5, 10 inches

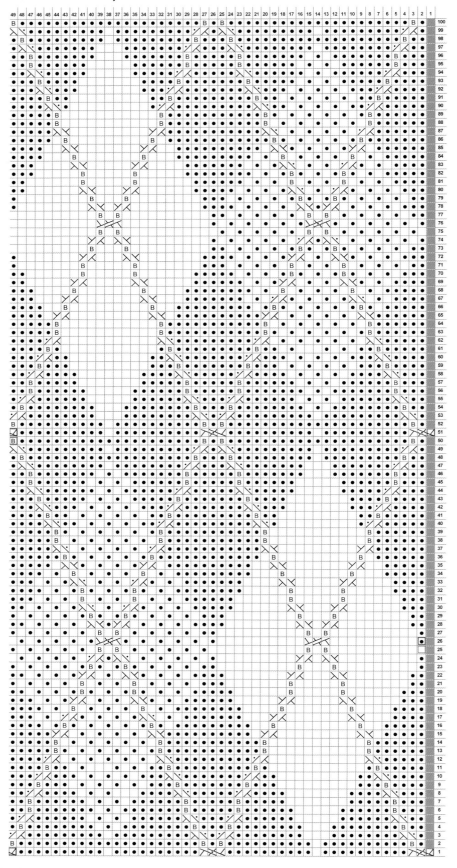

Instep Chart - 9.5, 10 inches

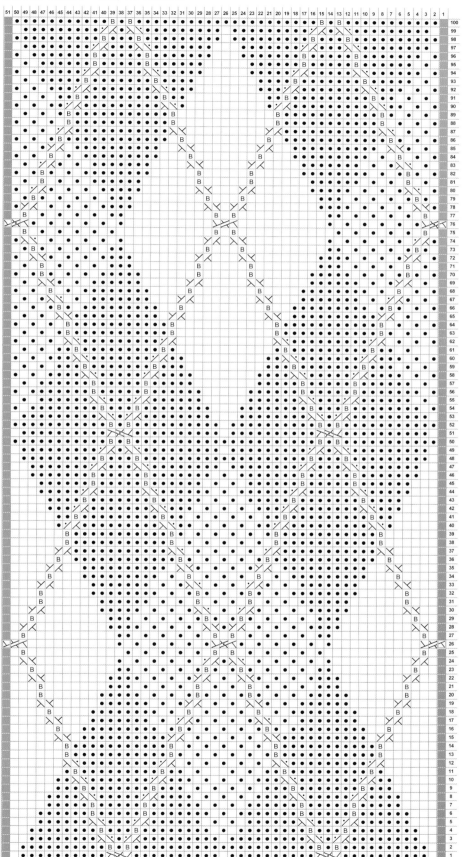

Main Chart - 10.5 inches

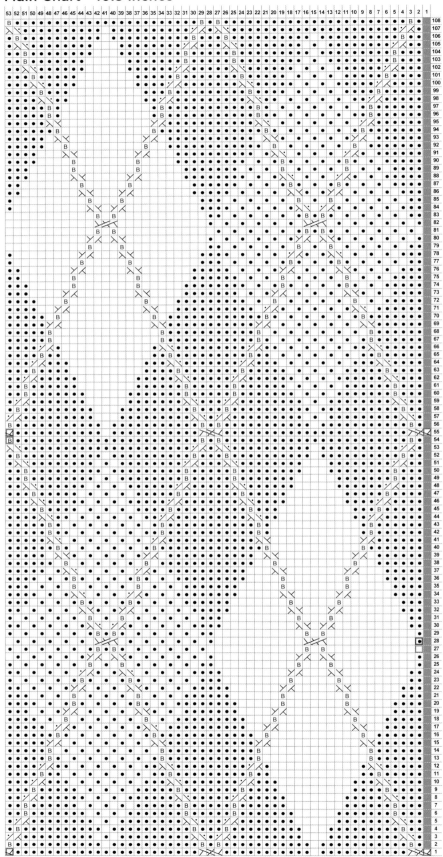

Instep Chart - 10.5 inches

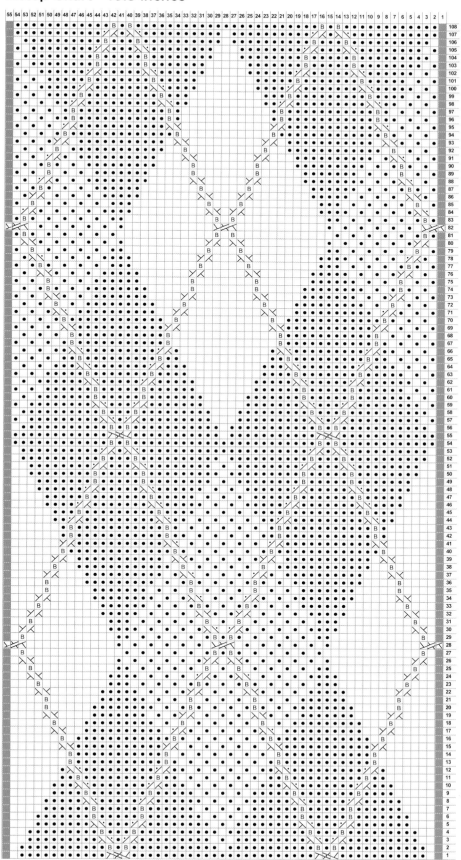

HYGGELIG CUSHION

by Nina Talbot

FINISHED MEASUREMENTS
19″ square, to fit 20″ pillow insert

YARN
Knit Picks The Big Cozy (super bulky weight, 55% Superfine Alpaca, 45% Peruvian Highland Wool; 44 yards/100g): MC Bare 26483, 5 skeins; C1 Cobblestone Heather, 26484, 2 skeins

NEEDLES
US 15 (10mm) circular needles, or size to obtain gauge

NOTIONS
Yarn Needle
Sewing Needle

20″ Square Pillow Insert
18″ Non-Separating Zipper
Small amount of sock yarn in a similar color to MC for seaming
Sewing thread in a similar color to MC for sewing in zipper

GAUGE
8 sts and 13 rows = 4″ in stockinette stitch blocked
6 sts and 20 rows = 4″ in Bi-Color Honeycomb Brioche Stitch Pattern, blocked

Hyggelig Cushion

Notes:

Hyggelig translates from Danish as cozy, comfortable, and homey. If you are looking for a great project that will bring a happy warm feeling to your home, look no further! Knit in The Big Cozy in contrasting colors, this soft cushion cover will add comfort and timeless style to your sofa, bed, or favorite chair. A super bulky yarn makes this Hyggelig cover a quick-to-make keepsake.

The front side features a lofty Bi-Color Honeycomb Brioche stitch, and the back is knit in solid color stockinette. The front and back are worked flat and seamed together. A zipper is added to one side to allow for easy washing.

When changing colors, carry the new yarn along the edge over the old yarn to avoid holes in fabric.

Turn Work
Flip the piece over and work on the reverse side as you normally would when knitting rows with circular needles.

Slide Work
Keep the same side facing you, pushing all the sts to the right end of the circular needles. Without turning the work, start the new row.

Yarn Over Slip (YOS)
Bring yarn forward, SL 1 st P-wise, bring yarn over right needle.

Brioche Knit 2 tog (BK2tog)
Knit the next st tog with its paired YO.

Brioche Purl 2 tog (BP2tog)
Purl the next st together with its paired YO.

Bi-Color Honeycomb Brioche Stitch Pattern
(worked flat over 31 sts)
Setup Row (WS): Turn work and with MC, *K1, YOS; rep from * to last st, K1.
Row 1 (RS): Turn work and with C1, SL1 WYIB, *K1, SL YO WYIB, K1; rep from * to last 2 sts, K1, SL YO WYIB, SL1 WYIB.
Row 2 (RS): Slide work and with MC, K1, *BP2tog, YOS; rep from * to last 2 sts, BP2tog, K1.
Row 3 (WS): Turn work and with C1, SL1 WYIF, P1, *SL YO WYIF, P2; rep from * to last st, SL1 WYIF.
Row 4 (WS): Slide work and with MC, K1, *YOS, BK2tog; rep from * to last 2 sts, YOS, K1.
Rep Rows 1-4 for pattern.

Mattress Stitch
A tutorial for the Mattress St can be found at https://tutorials.knitpicks.com/mattress-stitch/.

DIRECTIONS

Back
The back square is worked flat in St st with a garter edge.
With MC, loosely CO 39 sts.
Setup Row (WS): Turn work and K1, P37, K1.
Row 1 (RS): K across.
Row 2 (WS): K1, P37, K1.
Rep Rows 1-2 31 times, or until piece measures 19" from the CO edge.
Loosely BO all sts K-wise.

Front
The front square is worked flat in Bi-Color Honeycomb Brioche Stitch Pattern.
With MC, loosely CO 31 sts.
Work the Setup Row, then work Rows 1-4 of the Bi-Color Honeycomb Brioche Stitch Pattern.
Rep Rows 1-4 another 22 times, or until piece measures 19" from the CO edge, ending with Row 4.
With MC, loosely BO all sts K-wise. When binding off, treat the st with its paired YO as one st, knitting the st and its paired YO tog.

Finishing
Weave in ends, wash, and block each piece to measurements.

Because of the thickness and the softly spun nature of The Big Cozy yarn, it is preferable to seam with a firmly spun, thinner yarn, such as sock yarn, in a similar color.

First, attach a side zipper. Center and pin the zipper along the CO edges of the front and back pieces, leaving 0.5" on both sides. With a sewing needle and thread the same color as the yarn, back stitch the zipper into place. Work with the RS of knitted fabric facing you.
When the zipper is in place, lay front and back pieces RS up and use sock yarn and Mattress stitch to seam both pieces together. Start with closing the gap on one side of the zipper and continue seaming around to the other side.
Weave in ends and insert a pillow form.

JOURNEY'S END BLANKET

by Luise O'Neill

FINISHED MEASUREMENTS
48″ x 48 (60)″

YARN
Knit Picks Simply Alpaca (Aran weight, 100% Superfine Alpaca; 246 yards/100g): Alonzo 27489, 6 (7) hanks

NEEDLES
US 10 (6mm) 32″ long or longer circular needle, or size to obtain gauge

NOTIONS
Yarn Needle

GAUGE
16 sts and 32 rows = 4″ over Main Pattern, blocked
13 sts and 32 rows = 4″ in garter stitch, blocked

Journey's End

Notes:

A Journey's End is a comforting and calming instrumental tune by modern-day composer Peter Gundry. What better way to relax at the end of a long day, when the cold winds of winter swirl the snow throughout the landscape, than by listening to your favorite music and cuddling up under this coziest of blankets? The pattern comes in two sizes, so whether you just want a quick lap throw (48" x 48") to keep the chill at bay or want to totally wrap yourself in the lavish warmth of the larger 48" x 60" blanket, the pure luxury of this alpaca yarn will make you wish for more of those stormy winter days!

The blanket begins and ends with a garter stitch border; narrow garter stitch edges that begin (right edge) and end (left edge) with a slipped-stitch mock I-cord create beautifully rounded sides. The center of the blanket is worked in a magical pattern that only requires the knitter to be able to knit and slip stitches to create this fabulous reversible piece.

Blocking Notes: Wet the blanket thoroughly, gently squeeze out as much moisture as possible, and then roll it in toweling to remove excess moisture. Remove from toweling and gently pull the blanket both horizontally and vertically to set the stitches, then lay flat to dry; do not pin. Shaping the damp blanket to approximately 50" x 51 (64)" will result in the stated size as this stitch pattern will contract slightly during drying, which gives this blanket its luxurious texture.

Garter Stitch (worked flat over any number of sts)
All Rows: Knit all.

DIRECTIONS
Bottom Border
CO 150 sts.
Row 1 (RS): K1, SL1 WYIF, K to last 2 sts, SL1 WYIF, K1.
Row 2 (WS): SL1 WYIF, K1, SL1 WYIF, K to last 3 sts, SL1 WYIF, K1, SL1 WYIF.
Rows 3-8: Rep Rows 1-2 three more times.
Row 9: Rep Row 1.
Row 10 (Inc): SL1 WYIF, K1, SL1 WYIF, *K4, M1; rep from * to last 7 sts, K4, SL1 WYIF, K1, SL1 WYIF. 185 sts.

Main Pattern
Row 1 (RS): K1, SL1 WYIF, K to last 2 sts, SL1 WYIF, K1.
Row 2 (WS): SL1 WYIF, K1, SL1 WYIF, K to last 3 sts, SL1 WYIF, K1, SL1 WYIF.
Row 3: K1, SL1 WYIF, K4, *SL1, K1; rep from * to last 5 sts, K3, SL1 WYIF, K1.
Row 4: SL1 WYIF, K1, SL1 WYIF, K3, *SL1 WYIF, K1; rep from * to last 5 sts, K2, SL1 WYIF, K1, SL1 WYIF.
Row 5: Rep Row 1.
Row 6: Rep Row 2.
Row 7: K1, SL1 WYIF, K5, *SL1, K1; rep from * to last 6 sts, K4, SL1 WYIF, K1.
Row 8: SL1 WYIF, K1, SL1 WYIF, K4, *SL1 WYIF, K1; rep from * to last 6 sts, K3, SL1 WYIF, K1, SL1 WYIF.
Rep Rows 1-8 until work measures 46.75 (58.75)" from the CO edge, ending having completed a Row 8.
Next Row (RS): K1, SL1 WYIF, K to last 2 sts, SL1 WYIF, K1.
Next Row (Dec - WS): SL1 WYIF, K1, SL1 WYIF, K5, K2tog, *K3, K2tog; rep from * to last 5 sts, K2, SL1 WYIF, K1, SL1 WYIF. 150 sts.

Top Border
Row 1 (RS): K1, SL1 WYIF, K to last 2 sts, SL1 WYIF, K1.
Row 2 (WS): SL1 WYIF, K1, SL1 WYIF, K to last 3 sts, SL1 WYIF, K1, SL1 WYIF.
Rows 3-8: Rep Rows 1-2 three more times.
Row 9: Rep Row 1.
With WS facing, BO K-wise.

Finishing
Weave in ends, wash, and block (see notes).

LOUNGE SWEATER

by Violet LeBeaux

FINISHED MEASUREMENTS

38.75 (41.25, 46, 50.75, 53.25, 58)"
finished waist/bust measurement

YARN

Knit Picks Comfy (worsted weight,
75% Pima Cotton, 25% Acrylic; 109
yards/50g): Sea Foam 24153, 11 (12,
14, 16, 17, 19) skeins

NEEDLES

US 7 (4.5mm) DPNs and 16" circular
needles, or 32" or longer circular needles
for Magic Loop technique, or two

24" circular needles for two circulars
technique, or size to obtain gauge

NOTIONS

Yarn Needle
Stitch Markers
Scrap Yarn or Stitch Holder

GAUGE

20 sts and 28 rows = 4" in stockinette
stitch, blocked
20 sts and 28 rows = 4" in ribbed st,
blocked

Lounge Sweater

Notes:

Lounge is a comfortably oversized sweater which is perfect for rainy days spent indoors with a cup of tea and a good TV show. The diagonal rib creates a bias fabric that flatters the figure and sits well over curves. It features a rounded split hem that moves upward into diagonal stripes that gradually become further apart as they head towards the top of the sweater. The collar and cuffs feature a folded rib adding to the squishy texture.

Construction of Lounge is bottom up for minimal seaming, and it switches between working flat and in the round.

Blocking

The nature of the ribbing at the bottom of this sweater means it requires blocking to open it up and achieve the listed measurements. Gentle steam blocking or wet blocking is recommended for best results. Additionally, to keep the length on the side seams and prevent drooping, a piece of yarn or ribbon can be threaded down the sides and secured, or a row of crochet chain can be added for reinforcement.

DR (Decrease Right)

Dec 1 st using a right leaning dec. To know which dec to use, look at the second st on the LH needle. If the st is a K then K2tog, if the next st is a P then P2tog.

DL (Decrease Left)

Dec 1 st using a left leaning dec. To know which dec to use, look at the next st on the LH needle. If the next st is a P then SSP, if the next st is a K then SSK.

Make 1 Knit Left (M1L)

From the front, insert the LH needle under the bar between the previous st and next st. K TBL of the bar.

Make 1 Knit Right (M1R)

From the back, insert the LH needle under the bar between the previous st and next st. K TFL of the bar.

Make 1 Purl Left (M1LP)

From the front, insert the LH needle under the bar between the previous st and next st. P TBL of the bar.

Make 1 Purl Right (M1RP)

From the back, insert the LH needle under the bar between the previous st and next st. P TFL of the bar.

Work as Established

Cont the row/rnd working every st in the same way it was worked the previous row. If the st was K in the row below, K again. If the st was P in the row below, P again. If the st was SL in the previous row, K. There are no increases or decreases in these rows, only K and P.

K2, P2 Ribbing (in the rnd over multiples of 4 sts)

All Rnds: *K2, P2; rep from * to end of rnd.

DIRECTIONS

Body

The body section is worked from the bottom up.

Hem Ribbing

This section is worked flat, partially in short rows, and creates the curved ribbing at the hem of the sweater.

Loosely CO 97 (103, 115, 127, 133, 145) sts.

Row 1 (RS): *K1, P2; rep from * to last st, K1, turn.

Row 2 (WS) Work as established to end, turn.

Rows 3-4: Work as established until 2 sts remain, turn.

Rows 5-6: Work as established until 4 sts remain, turn.

Rows 7-8: Work as established until 6 sts remain, turn.

Rows 9-10: Work as established until 8 sts remain, turn.

Rows 11-12: Work as established to end.

Place these Front hem sts on holder and rep the section once more to create the Back hem. Do not break yarn or place Back sts on holder.

Body

This section of the sweater features the diagonal rib lines and is worked in the rnd. Add held Front Hem Ribbing sts from the holder back to the needles, PM and join to work in the rnd. 194 (206, 230, 254, 266, 290) sts.

Set Up Rnd: Work 48 (51, 57, 63, 66, 72) sts as established, PM, K1, PM, work 48 (51, 57, 63, 66, 72) sts as established, PM, work 48 (51, 57, 63, 66, 72) sts as established, PM, K1, PM, work remaining 48 (51, 57, 63, 66, 72) sts to end as established.

Rnd 1: *SL1, DR, work as established to M, M1R, SM, K1, SM, M1L, work as established to 3 sts before M, DL, SL1, SM; rep from * to end.

Rnd 2: Work as established to end.

Rnd 3: *SL1, DR, work as established to M, M1RP, SM, K1, SM, M1LP, work as established to 3 sts before M, DL, SL1, SM; rep from * to end.

Rnd 4: Work as established to end.

Rnds 5-6: Rep Rnds 3-4 one more time.

Rnds 7-8: Rep Rnds 1-2.

Rnds 9-26: Rep Rnds 3-8 three more times.

Rnds 27-32: Rep Rnds 3-4 three times.

Rnds 33-34: Rep Rnds 1-2.

Rnds 35-40: Rep Rnds 3-4 three times.

Rnds 41-42: Rep Rnds 1-2.

Rnds 43-50: Rep Rnds 3-4 four times.

Rnds 51-52: Rep Rnds 1-2.

Rnds 53-62: Rep Rnds 3-4 five times.

Rnds 63-64: Rep Rnds 1-2.

Rnds 65-76: Rep Rnds 3-4 six times.

Rnds 77-78: Rep Rnds 1-2.

Rnds 79-92: Rep Rnds 3-4 seven times.

Rnds 93-94: Rep Rnds 1-2.

Rnds 95-110: Rep Rnds 3-4 eight times.

Rnds 111-112: Rep Rnds 1-2.

Rep Rnds 3-4 5 (7, 9, 11, 12, 14) more times OR until piece measures 19.25 (19.75, 20.25, 20.75, 21.25, 21.75)" in total length then move on to Upper Body section.

Upper Body

Divide the sts in half as follows: Front 97 (103, 115, 127, 133, 145) sts, Back 97 (103, 115, 127, 133, 145) sts. Place the Back sts on holder and work Upper Body Section over Front sts.

This section is knit flat and creates shaping for the sleeves. To lengthen the armholes, add additional rows to this section.
Row 1 (RS): K1, DR, DR, work as established to M, M1RP, SM, K1, SM, M1LP, work rib as established to 5 sts before end, DL, DL K1. 2 sts dec.
Row 2: Work as established to end.
Rep Rows 1-2 14 more times or until section measures approximately 4.25" from the start of the sleeve hole, ending on a WS row. 67 (73, 85, 97, 103, 115) sts.

With RS facing, divide sts as follows: Right Collar 33 (36, 42, 48, 51, 57) sts, Left Collar 34 (37, 43, 49, 52, 58) sts. Place the Left Collar sts on holder and move on to the Right Collar Section.

Right Neck Shaping

This section creates a rounded neckline and is worked flat.
Row 1 (RS): Work as established until 3 sts remain, DL, K1. 1 st dec.
Row 2: Work as established to end.
Rep Rows 1-2 12 more times. 20 (23, 29, 35, 38, 44) sts. Work as established for 0 (2, 4, 6, 8, 10) more rows OR until piece measures approximately 8 (8.25, 8.5, 9, 9.25, 9.5)" from the start of the arm hole.
BO all sts or if you prefer to graft the shoulder seam, place sts on hold.

Left Neck Shaping

This section creates a rounded neckline and is worked flat.
Place held 34 (37, 43, 49, 52, 58) Left Collar sts on the needles.
Row 1 (WS): Work as established until 4 sts remain, DR, DR. 2 sts dec.
Row 2: Work as established to end.
Row 3: Work as established until 3 sts remain, DR, P1. 1 st dec.
Row 4: Work as established to end.
Rep Rows 3-4 11 more times. 20 (23, 29, 35, 38, 44) sts. Work as established for 0 (2, 4, 6, 8, 10) more rows OR until piece measures approximately 8 (8.25, 8.5, 9, 9.25, 9.5)" from the start of the armhole.
BO all sts or if you prefer to graft the shoulder seam, place sts on hold.

Rep the Upper Body, Right Neck Shaping, and Left Neck Shaping sections again using the Back sts.
Graft or sew the shoulder seams together.

Sleeves

This section uses short rows for the sleeve cap and then continues by working the Sleeve Body in the rnd.

Sleeve Cap

If you have knit extra rows in the Upper Body sections to achieve the desired length, add one st to the PU number for every additional 2 rows added.

Set Up Rnd 1: Starting from the bottom of the armhole and working around, PU and K 80 (84, 84, 90, 90, 94) sts evenly and PM to indicate start of rnd.

Set Up Rnd 2: K all.

Short Row 1 (RS): K52 (54, 54, 57, 57, 59), turn.

Short Row 2 (WS): P24, turn.

Short Row 3: K to 1 st past previous gap, turn.

Short Row 4: P to 1 st past previous gap, turn.

Rep Short Rows 3-4 22 (24, 24, 27, 27, 29) more times.

Next RS Row: K all. 80 (84, 84, 90, 90, 94) sts.

Sleeve Body

This section is worked in the rnd, PM for beginning of rnd.

Rnd 1: K1, K2tog, K to 3 sts remaining, SSK, K1. 2 sts dec.

Rnds 2-6: K all.

Rep Rnds 1-6 16 more times then Rnd 1 1 (1, 1, 0, 0, 0) more time OR until section measures approximately 14.75" from

under arm, or approximately 1" shorter than desired length, and has a number of sts which is divisible by 4. 44 (48, 48, 56, 56, 60) sts.

Cuff

Rnds 1-14: Work in 2x2 Rib.

BO all sts loosely.

Fold Cuff section inwards in half and sew down along the inside of the first Ribbing Rnd.

Rep Sleeve Cap, Sleeve and Cuff sections for the other arm hole.

Collar

This section is worked in the rnd around the edge of the Front, Left/Right, and Back shaping sections, to form the ribbed collar.

PU and K 52 (60, 68, 76, 84, 92) sts around the collar and PM, join to work in the rnd.

Rnds 1-14: Work in 2x2 Rib.

BO all sts loosely,

Fold Collar section inwards in half and sew down along the inside of the first Ribbing Rnd.

Finishing

Weave in ends, wash, and block to diagram.

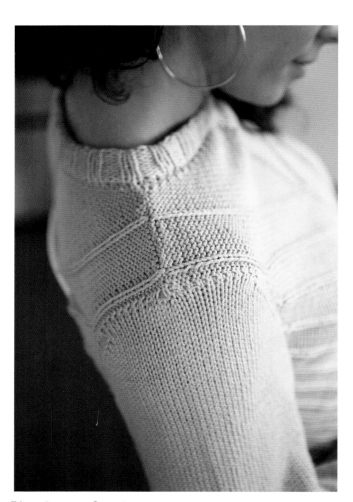

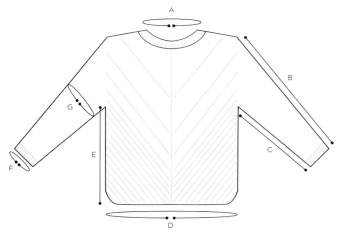

A: 10.5 (12, 13.5, 15.25, 16.75, 18.5)"
B: 23 (23.5, 23.5, 24.5, 24.5, 25)"
C: 15.75"
D: 38.75 (41.25, 46, 50.75, 53.25, 58)"
E: 19.25 (19.75, 20.25, 20.75, 21.25, 21.75)"
F: 8.75 (9.5, 9.5, 11.25, 11.25, 12)"
G: 15.5 (16.5, 16.5, 17.5, 17.5, 18.5)"

LUXURY LOUNGE

by Holli Yeoh

FINISHED MEASUREMENTS
41.75 (44.75, 47.75, 50.5, 55, 59.5, 62.5, 67, 71.5, 74.5)" finished bust measurement; garment is meant to be worn with approximately 10" of ease

YARN
Knit Picks Alpaca Cloud (fingering weight, 100% Superfine Alpaca; 440 yards/ 50g): Bennet 26886, 5 (6, 6, 6, 7, 7, 7, 8, 8, 9) hanks
Knit Picks Aloft Super Kid Mohair (lace weight, 72% Super Kid Mohair, 28% Silk; 200 yards/50g): Kenai 25755, 4 (5, 5, 5, 6, 6, 6, 7, 7, 7) balls

NEEDLES
US 7 (4.5mm) straight or circular needles, or size to obtain gauge
US 7 (4.5mm) 24" circular needle, or size to obtain gauge
US 3 (3.25mm) 24" circular needle, or 4 sizes smaller than needle to obtain gauge

US 5 (3.75mm) 24" circular needle, or 2 sizes smaller than needle to obtain gauge

NOTIONS
Yarn Needle
Removable or Locking Stitch Markers
Scrap Yarn or Stitch Holder

GAUGE
10.75 sts and 34 rows = 4" over Broken Fisherman's Rib pattern, holding a strand of each yarn together with US 7 (4.5mm) needles, blocked; (6 x 2-st reps = 4.5" and 17 x 2-row reps = 4")
11.75 sts and 38 rows = 4" over Broken Fisherman's Rib pattern, holding a strand of each yarn together with US 7 (4.5mm) needles, unblocked; (7 x 2-st reps = 4.75" and 19 x 2-row reps = 4")

Luxury Lounge

Notes:

Luxury fibers and a relaxed silhouette combine to make this your new favorite sweater. A simple broken fisherman's rib stitch creates the texture; a split hem in two lengths and plenty of positive ease create the modern, easygoing shape.

Holding a strand each of laceweight mohair and fingering weight alpaca together makes for an airy, lightweight fabric that traps a lot of air to keep you warm on the chilliest of winter days.

Worked bottom up and seamed, this sweater has short row shoulder shaping and a visible 3-Needle Bind Off to add design interest at the shoulders. But the real highlight is the generous cowl, which is worked in the round, bringing all that gorgeous softness up around your neck for full enjoyment.

The Broken Fisherman's Rib stitch pattern condenses the rows so only one row is visible (in the column of knit stitches) for every two rows worked. When counting rows, be sure to multiply by 2 to get an accurate row count.

All length measurements in pattern instructions are calculated with the *unblocked* row gauge of 9.5 rows/inch. The schematic and finished measurements reflect the blocked row gauge.

Knit 1 Below (K1B)
Knit into st directly below next st on needle, allowing next st to drop off needle.

Hem Pattern (worked flat over an even number of sts)
Row 1 (RS): SL 1 WYIF, *K1B, P1; rep from * to last st, K1.
Row 2 (WS): SL 1 WYIF, P to last st, K1.
Rep Rows 1 and 2 for Hem pattern.

Broken Fisherman's Rib Pattern (worked flat over an even number of sts)
Purl 1 row.
Row 1 (RS): K1, *K1B, P1; rep from * to last st, K1.
Row 2 (WS): Purl.
Rep Rows 1 and 2 for Broken Fisherman's Rib pattern.

Broken Fisherman's Rib Pattern (worked in the rnd over an even number of sts)
Rnd 1: Knit.
Rnd 2: *P1, K1B; rep from * to end of rnd.
Rep Rnds 1 and 2 for Broken Fisherman's Rib pattern.

German Short Rows
I favor this method when working short rows across a stitch pattern with knits and purls appearing on the same side, such as the Broken Fisherman's Rib. There is no need to fiddle with wrapping sts and then hiding the wrap later. Work to turning point; turn. WYIF, SL the first st P-wise. Bring yarn over the back of the right needle, pulling firmly to create a "double stitch" on the right needle. If the next st is a K st, leave the yarn at the back; if the next st is a P st, bring the yarn to the front between the needles. When it's time to work into the double st, knit both strands tog.

German Short Row (GSR)
The turning point (or gap) just before the double st created by the German short row technique.

Special Note: When working in the Broken Fisherman's Rib pattern, if the last st before turning is a K1B, replace it with K1.

Russian Bind Off
On a RS row, K1, *K1; without twisting them, return 2 sts just worked to the left needle then K2tog through the back of the sts; rep from * until all sts have been worked, and 1 st remains on right needle. Break yarn and pull through final st to secure. On a WS row, work P-wise.

Russian 3-Needle Bind Off
Hold two pieces of knitting with WS together, needles parallel and in left hand ready to be worked. Insert a third needle K-wise into the first st on each needle beginning with the front needle. Knit these two sts tog by wrapping yarn around needle and pulling a loop through both sts, allowing them to drop off their respective needles. *Work 2 tog as before, without twisting them, return 2 sts just worked to the left front needle then K2tog through the back of the sts; rep from * to end of row.

DIRECTIONS
Back
Ribbing
With US 5 (3.75mm) needles, loosely CO 112 (120, 128, 136, 148, 160, 168, 180, 192, 200) sts.
Row 1 (RS): SL 1 WYIF, *K1, P1; rep from * to last st, K1.
Rep last row twice more.
Dec Row (WS): SL 1 WYIF, K1, *P2tog, K2tog; rep from * to last 2 sts, P1, K1. 58 (62, 66, 70, 76, 82, 86, 92, 98, 102) sts.

Begin Hem Pattern
Change to US 7 (4.5mm) needles.
Row 1 (RS): SL 1 WYIF, *K1, P1; rep from * to last st, K1.
Beginning with Row 2 of Hem pattern, WE until piece measures 4.5" from CO edge, ending with a WS row.

Begin Broken Fisherman's Rib
Beginning with Row 1 of Broken Fisherman's Rib pattern, WE until piece measures 19.75 (20.25, 20.25, 20.75, 21, 21, 21.25, 21.5, 22, 22.5)" from CO edge, ending with a WS row.

Shoulder Shaping
The shoulders are shaped with short rows and worked in Broken Fisherman's Rib pattern throughout. The German Short Row method (see Notes) is recommended.
Short Rows 1 (RS) & 2 (WS): Work to last 3 sts, turn.
Short Rows 3 & 4: Work to 3 sts before last GSR, turn.
Rep Short Rows 3 & 4 an additional 1 (1, 2, 2, 3, 2, 4, 5, 8, 8) time(s) more.

Short Rows 5 & 6: Work to 2 sts before last GSR, turn.
Rep Short Rows 5 & 6 an additional 1 (2, 1, 2, 2, 5, 3, 3, 0, 1) time(s) more.
Next Row (RS): Work to end of row, working both strands of double sts tog, if using German Short Row method.
Next Row (WS): Work 15 (17, 18, 20, 23, 26, 28, 31, 34, 36) sts, using Russian Bind Off method, BO 28 (28, 30, 30, 30, 30, 30, 30, 30, 30) sts, work remaining 14 (16, 17, 19, 22, 25, 27, 30, 33, 35) sts. 15 (17, 18, 20, 23, 26, 28, 31, 34, 36) sts each shoulder. Place sts on holder.

Front

Ribbing and Hem
Work as for Back until hem measures 2.75″ from CO edge, ending with a WS row.

Begin Broken Fisherman's Rib
Begin with Row 1 of Broken Fisherman's Rib pattern, WE until piece measures 18 (18.25, 18.75, 19, 19.25, 19.25, 19.5, 19.75, 20.25, 20.5)″ from CO edge, ending with a RS row.
Next Row (WS): Work 22 (24, 25, 27, 30, 34, 36, 39, 42, 44) sts, PM, work 14 (14, 16, 16, 16, 14, 14, 14, 14, 14) sts, PM, work to end.

Shoulder Shaping
Sizes 55, 59.5, 62.5, 67, 71.5, 74.5″ Only
Work 1 RS row.

Sizes 59.5, 62.5, 67, 71.5, 74.5″ Only
Short Rows 1 (WS) & 2 (RS): Work to last 3 sts, turn.

Sizes 67, 71.5, 74.5″ Only
Short Rows 3 & 4: Work to 3 sts before last GSR, turn.
Rep Short Rows 3 & 4 – (–, –, –, –, –, –, 0, 0, 1) time(s) more.

Sizes 55, 59.5, 62.5, 67, 71.5, 74.5″ Only
Short Row 5 (WS): Work to 3 sts before last GSR or end of row, whichever is closer, turn.

All Sizes; Left Neck and Shoulder Shaping
Row 6 (RS): Work to 1 st before M, SL1. Cont on this set of sts only for left neckline and shoulder shaping. Place remaining sts on holder, if desired.

Sizes 41.75, 44.75, 47.75, 50.5″ Only
Row 7 (WS): SL2, pass first SL st over second SL st, work to end. 1 st dec.
Row 8 (RS): Work to 1 st before neck edge, SL 1.
Rep last 2 rows 1 (0, 0, 0, –, –, –, –, –, –) more time(s).

All Sizes
Row 9 (WS): SL2, pass first SL st over second SL st, work to 3 sts before last GSR or end of row, whichever is closer, turn. 1 st dec.
Row 10 and RS rows: Work to 1 st before neck edge, SL1.
Rep Row 9 every WS row, turning 3 sts before last GSR 2 (2, 3, 3, 3, 1, 3, 3, 6, 5) time(s) more, then turning 2 sts before last GSR 2 (3, 2, 3, 3, 6, 4, 4, 1, 2) time(s), ending with a WS row.

Next Row (RS): Work final 2 sts to end of row.
Next Row (WS): Work to end of row, working both strands of double sts tog, if using German Short Row method. 15 (17, 18, 20, 23, 26, 28, 31, 34, 36) sts.
Place shoulder sts on a holder. Break yarn, leaving a tail approximately 41 (45, 47, 52, 58, 65, 69, 76, 82, 87)″ long to be used later in a Russian 3-Needle Bind Off.

Right Neck and Shoulder Shaping
With RS facing, transfer center 14 (14, 16, 16, 16, 14, 14, 14, 14, 14) sts to a holder.

Sizes 41.75, 44.75, 47.75, 50.5″ Only
Row 1 (RS): Join yarn at neck edge beside held sts, work to end of row. Continue on this set of sts only for right neckline and shoulder shaping.

Sizes 41.75, 44.75, 47.75" Only
Row 2 (WS): Work to 1 st before neck edge, SL1.
Row 3: SL2, pass first SL over second SL st, work to end. 1 st dec.
Rep last 2 rows 1 (0, 0, –, –, –, –, –, –) more time(s).

Sizes 55, 59.5, 62.5, 67, 71.5, 74.5" Only
Row 4 (RS): Join yarn at neck edge beside held sts, work to 3 sts before last GSR or end of row, whichever is closer, turn. Continue on this set of sts only for right neckline and shoulder shaping.

All Sizes
Row 5 and WS rows: Work to 1 st before neck edge, SL1.
Short Row 6: SL2, pass first SL st over second SL st, work to 3 sts before last GSR or end of row, whichever is closer, turn. 1 st dec.
Rep Row 6 every RS row, turning 3 sts before last GSR 2 (2, 3, 3, 3, 1, 3, 3, 6, 5) time(s) more, then turning 2 sts before last GSR 2 (3, 2, 3, 3, 6, 4, 4, 1, 2) time(s), ending with a RS row.
Next Row (WS): Work final 2 sts to end of row.
Next Row (RS): Work to end of row, working both strands of double sts tog, if using German Short Row method. 15 (17, 18, 20, 23, 26, 28, 31, 34, 36) sts.
Place shoulder sts on a holder. Break yarn, leaving a tail approximately 41 (45, 47, 52, 58, 65, 69, 76, 82, 87)" long.

Sleeves (make 2 the same)
Ribbing
With US 5 (3.75mm) needles, loosely CO 44 (48, 48, 48, 48, 52, 52, 52, 52, 52) sts.
Row 1 (RS): K1, *K1, P1; rep from * to last st, K1.
Row 2 (WS): P1, *K1, P1; rep from * to last st, P1.
Row 3: Rep Row 1.
Dec Row (WS): P1, K1, *P2tog, K2tog; rep from * to last 2 sts, P2. 24 (26, 26, 26, 26, 28, 28, 28, 28, 28) sts.

Begin Broken Fisherman's Rib
Change to US 7 (4.5mm) needles.
Row 1 (RS): K1, *K1, P1; rep from * to last st, K1.
Beginning with Row 2 of Broken Fisherman's Rib pattern, WE until piece measures 2.75", ending with a WS row.

Sleeve Shaping
Inc Row (RS): K1, K1B, P1, (K1B, YO, K1B) into next st, work in pattern to last 5 sts, (K1B, YO, K1B) into next st, P1, K1B, P1, K1. 4 sts inc.
Rep Inc rnd every 58th (60th, 58th, 40th, 38th, 34th, 32nd, 30th, 20th, 18th) row 1 (1, 1, 2, 2, 2, 2, 2, 3, 3) more time(s). 32 (34, 34, 38, 38, 40, 40, 40, 44, 44) sts.
WE until sleeve measures 17 (17.25, 17.25, 17.5, 17, 16, 15.25, 14.75, 14, 13)" from beginning, ending with a WS row.
Using Russian Bind Off method, BO all sts.

Finishing

Wash and gently block pieces to schematic measurements. Holding WS together, join left shoulder seam using Russian 3-Needle Bind Off, working from armhole edge towards neck edge. Join right shoulder seam working P-wise from armhole edge to neck edge.

Place markers 6 (6.25, 6.25, 6.5, 6.75, 6.75, 7, 7.25, 7.5, 7.75)" down from each side of shoulder seams on selvage edges of Front and Back. Sew Sleeves between markers (taking care not to alter gauge of sleeve top), matching the center of the sleeve top with the shoulder seam. Using Mattress stitch, sew sleeve seams.

Place markers 5" up from each side of lower hem on selvage edges of Back and 3" up on Front. Sew side seams from markers to armhole.

Cowl Neck

With RS facing and US 3 (3.25mm) circular needle, PU and K 7 (7, 7, 7, 7, 8, 8, 8, 8, 8) sts on left Front neck from shoulder to Front neck BO, K16 (16, 18, 18, 18, 16, 16, 16, 16, 16) sts along Front center held sts, PU and K 7 (7, 7, 7, 7, 8, 8, 8, 8, 8) sts along right Front neck to shoulder, PU and K 30 (30, 32, 32, 32, 32, 32, 32, 32, 32) sts along Back neck. 60 (60, 64, 64, 64, 64, 64, 64, 64, 64) sts. PM for end of rnd.

Carefully turn pullover inside out through center of needle so WS of garment is facing. This is the RS of cowl. Work all rnds with this side facing.

Next Rnd: K2, PM, K3, PM, K21 (21, 23, 23, 23, 23, 23, 23, 23, 23), PM, K3, PM, K to end of rnd. 4 shaping markers.

Beginning with Rnd 2 of Broken Fisherman's Rib (in-the-rnd) pattern, WE until cowl measures 2", ending with a K rnd.

Inc Rnd: *Work to 1 st before next M, (K1B, YO, K1B) into next st, work to next M, (K1B, YO, K1B) into next st; rep from * once more, work to end of rnd. 8 sts inc.

Work even until cowl measures 2.75" from neckline.

Change to US 5 (3.75mm) needle. WE until cowl measures 4.5 " from neckline.

Change to US 7 (4.5mm) needle. WE until cowl measures 5.5" from neckline, ending with a K rnd.

Rep Inc Rnd once more. 76 (76, 80, 80, 80, 80, 80, 80, 80, 80) sts.

WE until cowl measures 7.25" from neckline, ending with a K rnd.

Using Russian Bind Off method, BO all sts.

Block cowl neck either by steaming it or gently washing the whole garment and laying flat to dry.

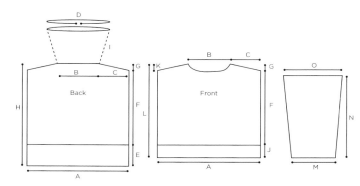

A: 21.5 (23, 24.5, 26, 28.25, 30.5, 32, 34.25, 36.5, 38)"
B: 10.5 (10.5, 11.25, 11.25, 11.25, 11.25, 11.25, 11.25, 11.25, 11.25)"
C: 5 (5.75, 6.25, 6.75, 7.75, 8.75, 9.5, 10.5, 11.5, 12.25)"
D: 28.25 (28.25, 29.75, 29.75, 29.75, 29.75, 29.75, 29.75, 29.75, 29.75)"
E: 5"
F: 18.5 (19, 19.5, 20, 20.5, 21, 21.5, 22, 22.5, 23)"
G: 1.5 (1.75, 1.75, 2, 2, 2.5, 2.5, 2.75, 2.75, 3)"
H: 23.5 (24, 24.5, 25, 25.5, 26, 26.5, 27, 27.5, 28)"
I: 8.75"
J: 3"
K: 1.75 (1.75, 1.75, 1.75, 1.75, 2, 2, 2, 2, 2)"
L: 21.5 (22, 22.5, 23, 23.5, 24, 24.5, 25, 25.5, 26)"
M: 9 (9.75, 9.75, 9.75, 9.75, 10.5, 10.5, 10.5, 10.5, 10.5)"
N: 19 (19.25, 19.25, 19.5, 19, 18, 17, 16.5, 15.75, 14.5)"
O: 12 (12.75, 12.75, 14.25, 14.25, 15, 15, 15, 16.25, 16.25)"

...to relax.

LYRA SWEATER

by Sue Gleave

FINISHED MEASUREMENTS

38 (42, 46, 50, 54, 58, 62, 66)" finished bust measurement; sweater is meant to be worn with 4-6" of ease

YARN

Knit Picks Andean Treasure (sport weight, 100% Baby Alpaca; 110 yards/ 50g): Royal Heather 25564, 12 (13, 14, 15, 16, 17, 18, 19) balls

NEEDLES

US 10 (6mm) straight or circular needles, or size to obtain gauge

US 9 (5.5mm) DPNs for I-cord, or one size smaller than size to obtain gauge

NOTIONS

Yarn Needle
Stitch Markers
Scrap Yarn or Stitch Holder

GAUGE

20 sts and 20 rows = 4" over Basketweave Pattern, blocked

Lyra Sweater

Notes:

When the snow's falling and the north wind's blowing, you need a sweater to curl up in by the fire and help you enjoy the season. To everything there is a season, and the art is to find the things that make it special to you.

The Lyra Sweater is a cozy garment, worked flat from the bottom up with a gently curved hem and a back that goes slightly lower than the front. It uses twisted stitches to create a woven texture that is very luxurious and knits up quickly on largish needles. The sleeves are worked in a similar fashion, and the cuffs and neck are finished with a narrow applied I-cord.

Make sure that you swatch this stitch pattern and follow the directions precisely; the K1 TBL is essential to achieve the Basketweave Pattern.

Lyra Basketweave Pattern (flat over an even number of sts)
Row 1 (RS): K1, *insert RH needle from back to front between first and second sts and K second st TBL, K first st then SL both sts off LH needle tog; rep from * to last st, K1.
Row 2 (WS): *Skip first st but leave on LH needle, P second st, P first st, then SL both sts off LH needle tog; rep from * end.
Rep Rows 1-2 for pattern.

DIRECTIONS
Front
The body is worked in two pieces, from the bottom up.

Lower Body, Dipped Hem
CO 68 (78, 84, 94, 100, 110, 116, 126) sts.
Hem Increase Row 1 (RS): K1, KFB twice, work Basketweave Pattern Row 1 to last 3 sts, KFB twice, K1. 4 sts inc.
Hem Increase Row 2 (WS): P1, work Basketweave Pattern Row 2 to last st, P1.
Work Rows 1 and 2 a total of 7 (7, 8, 8, 9, 9, 10, 10) times. 96 (106, 116, 126, 136, 146, 156, 166) sts.
Next Row (RS): K1, work Basketweave Pattern Row 1 to last st, K1.
Next Row (WS): P1, work Basketweave Pattern Row 2 to last st, P1.
Work these 2 rows a total of 7 (7, 7, 8, 8, 8, 9, 9) times.

Main Body
Row 1 (RS): P3, work Basketweave Pattern Row 1 to last 3 sts, P3.
Row 2 (WS): K3, work Basketweave Pattern Row 2 to last 3 sts, K3.
Work these 2 rows a total of 35 (37, 37, 36, 36, 35, 35, 35) times.

Divide for Shoulders, Shape Neck
Row 1 (RS): P3, work in pattern for 34 (38, 40, 44, 48, 54, 58, 62) sts for Left Shoulder, BO 22 (24, 30, 32, 34, 32, 34, 36) sts, work 34 (38, 40, 44, 48, 54, 58, 62) sts for Right Shoulder in pattern to last 3 sts, P3. Put Left Shoulder sts on st holder and work Right Shoulder.

Right Shoulder
Row 2 (WS) and all WS Rows: K3, work Basketweave Pattern Row 2 to end. 37 (41, 43, 47, 51, 57, 61, 65) sts.
Row 3 (RS): BO 2 sts, work in pattern to last 3 sts, P3. 35 (39, 41, 45, 49, 55, 59, 63) sts.
Row 5: BO 2 sts, work in pattern to last 3 sts, P3. 33 (37, 39, 43, 47, 53, 57, 61) sts.
Row 7: BO 2 sts, work in pattern to last 3 sts, P3. 31 (35, 37, 41, 45, 51, 55, 59) sts.
Row 9: BO 2 sts, work in pattern to last 3 sts, P3. 29 (33, 35, 39, 43, 49, 53, 57) sts.
Row 11: BO 2 sts, work in pattern to last 3 sts, P3. 27 (31, 33, 37, 41, 47, 51, 55) sts.
Row 13: BO 0 (0, 0, 2, 2, 2, 2, 2) sts, work in pattern to last 3 sts, P3. 27 (31, 33, 35, 39, 45, 49, 53) sts.
Row 15: BO 0 (0, 0, 0, 2, 2, 2, 2) sts, work in pattern to last 3 sts, P3. 27 (31, 33, 35, 37, 43, 47, 51) sts.
Row 16: K3, work Basketweave Pattern Row 2 to end.

Size 38, 42 & 46" Next Row: BO all sts.

Sizes 50 & 54" Only
Row 17: Work in pattern to last 3 sts, P3.
Row 19: Work in pattern to last 3 sts, P3.
Row 20: K3, work Basketweave Pattern Row 2 to end.
Next Row: BO all sts.

Sizes 58, 62, & 66" Only
Row 17: BO - (-, -, -, -, 2, 2, 2) sts, work in pattern to last 3 sts, P3. - (-, -, -, -, 41, 45, 49) sts.
Row 19: BO - (-, -, -, -, 0, 2, 2) sts, work in pattern to last 3 sts, P3. - (-, -, -, -, 41, 43, 47) sts.
Row 21: Work in pattern to last 3 sts, P3.
Row 22: K3, work Basketweave Pattern Row 2 to end.
Next Row: BO all sts.

Left Shoulder
Re-join the yarn to work the Left Shoulder sts with WS facing.
Row 2 (WS): BO 2 sts, work in pattern to last 3 sts, K3. 35 (39, 41, 45, 49, 55, 59, 63) sts.
Row 3 and all RS Rows: P3, work Basketweave Pattern Row 1 to end.
Row 4 BO 2 sts, work in pattern to last 3 sts, K3. 33 (37, 39, 43, 47, 53, 57, 61) sts.
Row 6: BO 2 sts, work in pattern to last 3 sts, K3. 31 (35, 37, 41, 45, 51, 55, 59) sts.
Row 8: BO 2 sts, work in pattern to last 3 sts, K3. 29 (33, 35, 39, 43, 49, 53, 57) sts.
Row 10: BO 2 sts, work in pattern to last 3 sts, K3. 27 (31, 33, 37, 41, 47, 51, 55) sts.
Row 12: BO 0 (0, 0, 2, 2, 2, 2, 2) sts, work in pattern to last 3 sts, K3. 27 (31, 33, 35, 39, 45, 49, 53) sts.
Row 14: BO 0 (0, 0, 0, 2, 2, 2, 2) sts, work in pattern to last 3 sts, K3. 27 (31, 33, 35, 37, 43, 47, 51) sts.
Row 16: BO 0 (0, 0, 0, 0, 2, 2, 2) sts, work in pattern to last 3 sts, K3. 27 (31, 33, 35, 37, 41, 45, 49) sts.

Sizes 38, 42 & 46" Next Row: BO all sts.

Sizes 50 & 54" Only
Row 18: Work in pattern to last 3 sts, K3.
Row 19: P3, work Basketweave Pattern Row 1 to end.
Row 20: Work in pattern to last 3 sts, K3.
Next Row: BO all sts.

Sizes 58, 62, & 66" Only
Row 18: BO - (-, -, -, -, 0, 2, 2) sts, work in pattern to last 3 sts, K3. - (-, -, -, -, 41, 43, 47) sts.
Row 20: Work in pattern to last 3 sts, K3.
Row 21: P3, work Basketweave Pattern Row 1 to end.
Row 22: Work in pattern to last 3 sts, K3.
Next Row: BO all sts.

Back

Lower Body, Dipped Hem
Work as for Front through Hem increases. 96 (106, 116, 126, 136, 146, 156, 166) sts.
Next Row: K1, work Basketweave Pattern Row 1 to last st, K1.
Next Row: P1, work Basketweave Pattern Row 2 to last st, P1.
Work these 2 rows a total of 14 (14, 14, 15, 15, 15, 16, 16) times.

Main Body
Row 1 (RS): P3, work Basketweave Pattern Row 1 to last 3 sts, P3.
Row 2 (WS): K3, work Basketweave Pattern Row 2 to last 3 sts, K3.
Work these 2 rows a total of 38 (40, 40, 39, 39, 39, 38, 39) times.

Divide for Shoulders and Shape Neck
Row 1 (RS): P3, work in pattern for 30 (34, 36, 40, 42, 46, 50, 54) sts for Right Shoulder, BO 30 (32, 38, 40, 46, 48, 50, 52) sts, work 30 (34, 36, 40, 42, 46, 50, 54) Left Shoulder sts in pattern to last 3 sts, P3. Put Right Shoulder sts on st holder and work Left Shoulder.

Left Shoulder
Row 2 (WS) and all WS Rows: K3, work Basketweave Pattern Row 2 to end. 33 (37, 39, 43, 45, 49, 53, 57) sts.
Row 3 (RS): BO 2 sts, work in pattern to last 3 sts, P3. 31 (35, 37, 41, 43, 47, 51, 55) sts.
Row 5: BO 2 sts, work in pattern to last 3 sts, P3. 29 (33, 35, 39, 41, 45, 49, 53) sts.
Row 7: BO 2 sts, work in pattern to last 3 sts, P3. 27 (31, 33, 37, 39, 43, 47, 51) sts.
Row 9: BO 0 (0, 0, 2, 2, 2, 2, 2) sts, work in pattern to last 3 sts, P3. 27 (31, 33, 35, 37, 41, 45, 49) sts.
Row 10: K3, work Basketweave Pattern Row 2 to end.

Sizes 38, 42 & 46" Next Row: BO all sts.

Sizes 50, 54, 58, 62, & 66" Only
Row 11: BO - (-, -, 0, 0, 0, 2, 2) sts, work in pattern to last 3 sts, P3. - (-, -, 35, 37, 41, 43, 47) sts.
Row 13: Work in pattern to last 3 sts, P3.
Row 14: K3, work Basketweave Pattern Row 2 to end.
Next Row: BO all sts.

Right Shoulder

Re-join the yarn to work the Right Shoulder sts with WS facing.

Row 2 (WS): BO 2 sts, work in pattern to last 3 sts, K3. 31 (35, 37, 41, 43, 47, 51, 55) sts.

Row 3 and all RS Rows: P3, work Basketweave Pattern Row 1 to end.

Row 4: BO 2 sts, work in pattern to last 3 sts, K3. 29 (33, 35, 39, 41, 45, 49, 53) sts.

Row 6: BO 2 sts, work in pattern to last 3 sts, K3. 27 (31, 33, 37, 39, 43, 47, 51) sts.

Row 8: BO 0 (0, 0, 2, 2, 2, 2, 2) sts, work in pattern to last 3 sts, K3. 27 (31, 33, 35, 37, 41, 45, 49) sts.

Row 9: P3, work Basketweave Pattern Row 2 to end.

Row 10: BO 0 (0, 0, 0, 0, 0, 2, 2) sts, work in pattern to last 3 sts, K3. 27 (31, 33, 35, 37, 41, 43, 47) sts.

Sizes 38, 42 & 46" Next Row: BO all sts.

Sizes 50, 54, 58, 62, & 66" Only

Row 12: BO - (-, -, 0, 0, 0, 2, 2) sts, work in pattern to last 3 sts, K3. - (-, -, 35, 37, 41, 43, 47) sts.

Row 14: Work in pattern to last 3 sts, K3. - (-, -, 35, 37, 41, 43, 47) sts.

Next Row: BO all sts.

Sleeves (make 2 the same)

The sleeves are worked flat from the wrists up. The sleeves are worked with a border of Rev St st. Maintain this border for the entire length of the sleeve, incorporating increases into the Basketweave Pattern. To maintain the pattern on rows where there has only been 1 st inc at each end of the row since the last full pattern row, add a K1 at each end of the Basketweave Pattern on RS rows and a P1 at each end on the WS rows.

CO 44 (46, 48. 50, 52, 52, 54, 56) sts.

Row 1 (RS): P2, work Basketweave Pattern Row 1 to last 2 sts, P2.

Row 2 (WS): K2, work Basketweave Pattern Row 2 to last 2 sts, K2.

Work these 2 Rows a total of 9 times.

Size 38, 42, 46 & 50" Only

Inc Row (RS): P2, M1 K-wise, work Basketweave Pattern Row 1 to last 2 sts, M1 K-wise, P2. 2 sts inc.

Work in pattern as established for 56 (60, 60, 60) more rows, at the same time working an Inc Row on next and then every fourth row. 72 (76, 78, 80, -, -, -, -) sts.

Size 54, 58, 62 & 66" Only

Inc Row (RS): P2, M1 K-wise, work Basketweave Pattern Row 1 to last 2 sts, M1 K-wise, P2. 2 sts inc.

Work in pattern as established for - (-, -, -, 18, 28, 40, 50) more rows, at the same time working an Inc Row on next and every second row. - (-, -, -, 70, 80, 94, 106) sts.

Work in pattern for - (-, -, -, 32, 24, 12, 0) more rows, working an Inc Row on next and every fourth row. - (-, -, -, 86, 92, 100, 106) sts.

All Sizes

WE until sleeve is 18.5 (18.5, 19, 19, 19.5, 19.5, 20, 20)" long, ending with a RS row.

Next Row: Purl across.

Next Row: BO all sts.

Finishing

Weave in ends, wash and block to diagram, noting that seam allowance sts are not included in measurements. Sew up seams using Mattress stitch, making sure that the bottom of the side seams start where the Rev St st border starts.

Neckband

Attach yarn at left shoulder of the neck; an I-cord will now be worked around the neck opening. All rows are worked with RS facing.

Setup Row (RS): With DPNs, CO 4 sts.

Row 1: K3, YO, SL1, K1 through edge of work, PSSO, pass YO over and off. Slide all sts from LH to RH side of DPN.

Rep Row 1 to work the I-cord, working 1 row for each st around the neck, then BO and fasten off yarn.

Cuffs

Attach yarn at sleeve seam; an I-cord will now be worked around the cuff, following directions given for the Neckband, working 1 row for each st around the bottom of the sleeve. All rows are worked with RS facing.

Neck and Cuff Finishing: Press the I-cord edging lightly and weave in loose ends to finish.

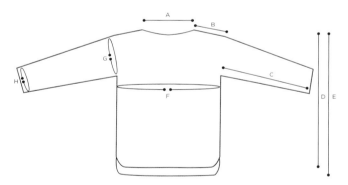

A: 8.5 (8.75, 10, 11.25, 12.5, 12.75, 14, 14.5)"
B: 5.25 (6, 6.5, 6.75, 7.25, 8, 8.5, 9.25)"
C: 19 (19, 19.5, 19.5, 20, 20, 20.5, 20.5)"
D: 23 (23.75, 24.25, 25, 25.5, 26.5, 26.5, 26.5)"
E: 25 (25.5, 26, 26.5, 27, 27.5, 27.5, 28)"
F: 38 (42, 46, 50, 54, 58, 62, 66)"
G: 14.5 (15.25, 15.5, 16, 17.25, 18.5, 20, 21.25)"
H: 8.75 (9.25, 9.5, 10, 10.5, 10.5, 10.75, 11.25)"

MYSA SOCKS

by Fabienne Gassmann

FINISHED MEASUREMENTS

8.75 (9.5, 10)" foot length, to fit shoe size 6 (8-8.5, 9.5-10); socks are meant to be worn with approximately 10% negative ease

YARN

Knit Picks Swish (worsted weight, 100% Fine Superwash Merino Wool; 110 yards/50g): Wonderland Heather 26067, 2 (2, 3) skeins

NEEDLES

US 6 (4mm) DPNs or longer circular needle for Magic Loop technique, or size to obtain gauge

NOTIONS

Yarn Needle
Stitch Markers

GAUGE

21 sts and 28 rows = 4" in stockinette stitch in the round, steam blocked

Mysa Socks

Notes:

Mysa Socks are cozy slipper socks for lounging around on those long, dark winter nights. Imagine coming home from a long walk in the cold, making yourself a cup of hot cocoa, and cuddling up on the sofa with toasty warm feet.

These socks are knitted top down with a traditional slip stitch heel flap and gusset construction. Knitted in worsted weight yarn, they are a quick make and an ideal first top down sock. The design feature that makes these socks special is the chunky cuff worked in rice stitch. The pattern comes with two versions, a fold-down and a stand-up cuff. Rice stitch is a bit more textured than garter stitch but almost as easy to knit; all that's needed is a twisted stitch every second stitch in every other row. The wrong side of rice stitch almost looks like a classic 1x1 Rib, a lovely surprise if the socks are worn with the cuff folded up.

Version 1: Fold-Down Cuff

Version 2: Stand-Up Cuff

Kitchener Stitch
A tutorial for the Kitchener Stitch can be found at https://tutorials.knitpicks.com/kitchener-stitch/.

Rice Stitch Pattern for Version 1 (in the rnd over multiple of 2 sts)
Rnd 1: (K1, P1 TBL) to end.
Rnd 2: K all.
Rep Rnds 1-2 for pattern.

Rice Stitch Pattern for Version 2 (in the rnd over multiple of 2 sts)
Rnd 1: (P1, K1 TBL) to end.
Rnd 2: P all.
Rep Rnds 1-2 for pattern.

Slip Stitch Pattern (worked flat over multiple of 2 sts plus 1)
Row 1 (RS): (SL1 K-wise, K1) to last st, SL last st K-wise.
Row 2 (WS): P across.
Rep Rows 1-2 for pattern.

DIRECTIONS
CO 40 (44, 48) sts for Version 1.
CO 38 (42, 46) sts for Version 2.

Cuff
Work appropriate Rice Stitch pattern for 25 rnds.
The last rnd should be Rnd 1 of the Rice Stitch Pattern.

Leg
Version 1
Rnd 1: K2tog, K17 (19, 2 1), K2tog, K to end. 38 (42, 46) sts.
Knit 29 rnds.

Version 2: Knit 5 rnds.

Heel Flap
SL 19 (21, 23) sts onto one needle for the heel. The remaining sts will not be worked during the heel flap or heel turn.
With RS facing, work Slip Stitch Pattern for 18 (20, 22) rows.

Heel Turn
Row 1 (RS): SL1 K-wise, K5, K2tog, K3 (5, 7), SSK, K5, SL1 K-wise. 17 (19, 21) sts.
Rows 2, 4, 6, 8, 10 (WS): P across.
Row 3: SL1 K-wise, K4, K2tog, K3 (5, 7), SSK, K4, SL1 K-wise. 15 (17, 19) sts.
Row 5: SL1 K-wise, K3, K2tog, K3 (5, 7), SSK, K3, SL1 K-wise. 13 (15, 17) sts.
Row 7: SL1 K-wise, K2, K2tog, K3 (5, 7), SSK, K2, SL1 K-wise. 11 (13, 15) sts.
Row 9: SL1 K-wise, K1, K2tog, K3 (5, 7), SSK, K1, SL1 K-wise. 9 (11, 13) sts.
Row 11: SL1 K-wise, K2tog, K3 (5, 7), SSK, SL1 K-wise. 7 (9, 11) sts.

Instep/Gusset
Start picking up sts along the LH side of the heel. Picking up sts twisted helps avoid holes along the join of the heel and first row of the gusset. PU and K 6 sts along the heel turn and 8 (9, 10) along the heel flap. K across instep and PU and K 8 (9, 10) sts on the other side of the heel. 14 (15, 16) total of new sts per side. 54 (58, 62) total sts.

Gusset Decrease
Rnd 1: K all.
Rnd 2: Work the last st of the sole and the first st of the instep as K2tog, the last st of the instep and the first st of the sole as SSK. 2 sts dec.
Work Rnds 1-2 eight times, until there are 38 (42, 46) sts on the needles.

Foot
Knit 22 (25, 28) rnds or until piece measures 1 (1.5, 2)″ shorter than desired length of foot.

Toe Shaping
Rnd 1 (Dec Rnd): Sole sts: K1, SSK, work to last 3 sts, K2tog, K1. Instep sts: K1, SSK, work to last 3 sts, K2tog, K1. 4 sts dec.
Rnd 2: K all.
Work Rnds 1-2 a total of 2 (3, 4) times, until 30 sts are left on the needles.
Work Rnd 1 only until 14 sts are left, 7 sts on the sole, 7 on the instep.
Move sts onto two needles, sole sts on one, instep sts on other. Holding needle 1 and needle 2 together, graft sts using Kitchener Stitch.

Finishing
Weave in ends, wash, and steam block.

Version 1

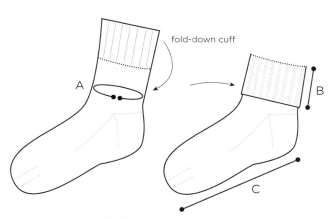

fold-down cuff

A: 7.5 (8.25, 9)"
B: 3"
C: 8.75 (9.5, 10)"
shoe size: 6 (8/8.5, 9.5/10)

Version 2

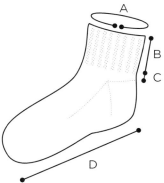

A: 7.5 (8.25, 9)"
B: 3"
C: 0.5"
D: 8.75 (9.5, 10)"
shoe size: 6 (8/8.5, 9.5/10)

STEEPED THROW

by Jenny Galusha-Luna

FINISHED MEASUREMENTS
47" x 54"

YARN
Knit Picks Brava (worsted weight, 100% Premium Acrylic; 218 yards/100g): MC White 25694, 9 skeins; C1 Persimmon 25715, 2 skeins; C2 Peacock 26127, 2 skeins

NEEDLES
US 8 (5mm) straight or 16" circular needles, plus 48" or longer circular needles for edging, or size to obtain gauge

NOTIONS
Yarn Needle

GAUGE
17 sts and 24 rows = 4" in stockinette stitch, lightly blocked (gauge for this project is not essential, but differences will affect finished size and yarn requirements)

Steeped Throw

Notes:

The Steeped Throw is a cozy blanket inspired by afternoon tea and cuddling with a good book. Simple color-blocking on mitered squares are reminiscent of tea bags steeping in a hot, comforting cup of tea. The mix of garter stitch and stockinette stitch creates a textured look without being too complicated. This blanket also uses just three colors: a neutral color and two contrasting colors. The neutral color invites you to make this your favorite blanket, while the contrasting colors help add a pop of visual interest without being too overpowering. Knitting this calming pattern will have you yearning for your favorite cozy spot.

Sk2p

Slip 1 stitch knitwise as if to knit, knit next 2 stitches, pass slip stitch over.

DIRECTIONS

Square

Make 21 squares in MC and C1, and 21 squares in MC and C2, for a total of 42 squares.

Use straight or shorter circular needles, and with MC, CO 59 sts.

Garter Stitch Section

Row 1 (RS): K28, Sk2p, K28. 57 sts.
Row 2 and all even numbered rows through Row 14 (WS): K across.
Row 3: K27, Sk2p, K27. 55 sts.
Row 5: K26, Sk2p, K26. 53 sts.
Row 7: K25, Sk2p, K25. 51 sts.
Row 9: K24, Sk2p, K24. 49 sts.
Row 11: K23, Sk2p, K23. 47 sts.
Row 13: K22, Sk2p, K22. 45 sts.

Stockinette Stitch Section

Row 15 (RS): K21, Sk2p, K21. 43 sts.
Row 16 and all even numbered rows through Row 28 (WS): K1, P to last st, K1.
Row 17: K20, Sk2p, K20. 41 sts.
Row 19: K19, Sk2p, K19. 39 sts.
Row 21: K18, Sk2p, K18. 37 sts.
Row 23: K17, Sk2p, K17. 35 sts.
Row 25: K16, Sk2p, K16. 33 sts.
Row 27: K15, Sk2p, K15. 31 sts.
Row 29: K14, Sk2p, K14. 29 sts.
Break off MC and switch to C1 (C2).

Garter Stitch Section

Row 30 (WS): With C1 (C2), K across. 29 sts.
Row 31 (RS): K13, Sk2p, K13. 27 sts.
Row 32 and all even numbered rows through Row 54 (WS): K across.
Row 33: K12, Sk2p, K12. 25 sts.
Row 35: K11, Sk2p, K11. 23 sts.
Row 37: K10, Sk2p, K10. 21 sts.
Row 39: K9, Sk2p, K9. 19 sts.
Row 41: K8, Sk2p, K8. 17 sts.
Row 43: K7, Sk2p, K7. 15 sts.
Row 45: K6, Sk2p, K6. 13 sts.
Row 47: K5, Sk2p, K5. 11 sts.
Row 49: K4, Sk2p, K4. 9 sts.
Row 51: K3, Sk2p, K3. 7 sts.
Row 53: K2, Sk2p, K2. 5 sts.
Row 55: K1, Sk2p, K1. 3 sts.
BO remaining 3 sts.

Finishing the Squares

Weave in ends. Lightly steam block squares to measure 7.5″ square. Seam squares together in 7 rows of 6 squares across, alternating the contrasting colors. Sew the 7 rows of squares together, keeping alternating pattern. Once all squares are sewn together, continue to Edging.

Edging

Use long circular needles to work the edging. Work one side of the throw at a time, picking up sts evenly along each edge so that it doesn't bunch (too few) or ruffle (too many). St count does not matter for edging.

Row 1 (RS): With MC, PU and K evenly along top edge of the blanket. Turn.
Rows 2-6: K across. Turn.
After Row 6, BO all sts with RS facing, but keep last BO st on needle. Turn throw 90 degrees in preparation to PU sts along the next edge.
Rep Rows 1-6 for each side of the throw.
After last edge has been worked, BO final st.

Finishing

Weave in remaining ends.

VINEYARD RUANA

by Megan Dial

FINISHED MEASUREMENTS
72.75" x 46"

YARN
Knit Picks Shimmer (bulky weight, 70% Baby Alpaca, 30% Mulberry Silk; 87 yards/100g): Bare 27615, 14 hanks

NEEDLES
US 10.5 (6.5mm) 32" or 40" circular needles, or size to obtain gauge

NOTIONS
Yarn Needle
Cable Needle
Stitch Holder, or spare 32" Circular Needle

GAUGE
12 sts and 15.5 rows = 4" in all stitch patterns, gently blocked

Vineyard Ruana

Notes:

Keep warm with a wistful look at the spring to come with this simple, easy-to-knit (but never boring) project. Heavenly to wrap up in during a winter storm or in front of a cozy fire, the Vineyard Ruana is the perfect companion to a cup of cocoa and a good book at the end of a long day. Made in a bulky yarn, it is quick and enjoyable to knit with just enough embellishment to make it stimulating and beautiful.

The Vineyard Ruana is a split rectangular wrap, worked flat from the short end and separated in the front. The 21 stitch wide and 22 row long Diamond Cable motif is worked over the length of the back, with Vine Lace edgings for the entire length of the sides.

Follow the charts on RS rows (odd numbers) from right to left, and on WS rows (even numbers) from left to right.

2/1 LC: SL 2 sts to CN, hold in front; K1; K2 from CN.
2/1 RC: SL 1 st to CN, hold in back; K2; K1 from CN.
2/1 LPC: SL 2 sts to CN, hold in front; P1; K2 from CN.
2/1 RPC: SL 1 st to CN, hold in back; K2; P1 from CN.
2/3 RC: SL 3 sts to CN, hold in back; K2, K3 from CN.

Odd Seed Stitch (worked flat over an odd number of sts)
Row 1: (K1, P1) to last st, K1.
Row 2: Rep Row 1.
Rep Rows 1-2 for pattern

Even Seed Stitch (worked flat over an even number of sts)
Row 1: (K1, P1) across.
Row 2: (P1, K1) across.
Rep Rows 1-2 for pattern.

DIRECTIONS
Back
Loosely CO 137 sts.
Work Rows 1-8 in Odd Seed Stitch.
Begin charts as follows and continue for 11 reps of Vine Charts and 7 concurrent reps of Diamond Chart (154 charted rows, 162 total rows):
RS Rows: Work Row 1 of Vine Right Chart, K34, work Diamond Chart, K34, work Vine Left Chart. Work in this order for all odd numbered rows.
WS Rows: Work Row 2 of Vine Left Chart, P34, work Diamond Chart, P34, work Vine Right Chart. Work in this order for all even numbered rows.

Neck
Row 163 (RS): Work Vine Right Chart, K28, work 33 sts in Odd Seed Stitch, K28, work Vine Left Chart.
Row 164 (WS): Work Vine Left Chart, P28, work 33 sts in Odd Seed Stitch, P28, work Vine Right Chart.
Rows 165-169: Rep Rows 163-164, ending with a Row 163.

Separate Front Sides

Row 170 (WS): Work Vine Left Chart, P28, (K1, P1) 3 times, BO 21 sts, (P1, K1) 3 times, P28, work Vine Right Chart. This will be on Row 8 of the charts, so Row 171 of both fronts (below) will start on Row 9 of charts.

Place left side of work on stitch holder or spare circular. Continue with Right Front.

Right Front

Row 171 and all RS rows: Continue Vine Right Chart, K28, (K1, P1) 3 times.

Row 172 and all WS rows: (P1, K1) 3 times, P28, work Vine Right Chart.

Continue to end of chart. Rep chart seven more times. (112 rows from start of Neck, 274 rows total.)

Rows 275-282: Work in Even Seed Stitch across. BO loosely. Continue to Left Front.

Left Front

Join yarn on RS.

Row 171 and all RS rows: (P1, K1) 3 times, K28, work Vine Left Chart.

Row 172 and all WS rows: Work Vine Left Chart, P28, (K1, P1) 3 times.

Continue to end of chart. Rep chart seven more times. (112 rows from start of Neck, 274 rows total.)

Row 275: Work Row 2 of Even Seed Stitch across.

Rows 276-282: Cont to work in Even Seed Stitch across. BO loosely.

Finishing

Weave in ends, wash, and block gently to diagram.

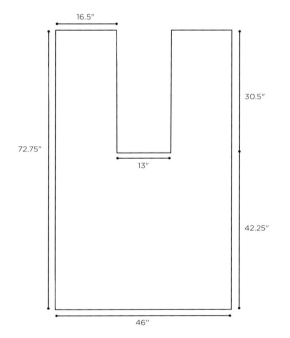

16.5″
30.5″
72.75″
13″
42.25″
46″

Vine Right Chart

Columns: 24 23 22 21 20 19 18 17 16 15 14 13 12 11 10 9 8 7 6 5 4 3 2 1
Rows: 14, 13, 12, 11, 10, 9, 8, 7, 6, 5, 4, 3, 2, 1

Vine Left Chart

Columns: 24 23 22 21 20 19 18 17 16 15 14 13 12 11 10 9 8 7 6 5 4 3 2 1
Rows: 14, 13, 12, 11, 10, 9, 8, 7, 6, 5, 4, 3, 2, 1

Diamond Chart

Columns: 21 20 19 18 17 16 15 14 13 12 11 10 9 8 7 6 5 4 3 2 1
Rows: 22, 21, 20, 19, 18, 17, 16, 15, 14, 13, 12, 11, 10, 9, 8, 7, 6, 5, 4, 3, 2, 1

Legend:

Knit
RS: knit stitch
WS: purl stitch

Purl
RS: purl stitch
WS: knit stitch

K2tog
RS: Knit two stitches together as one stitch
WS: Purl two stitches together

YO
Yarn over

SSK
RS: Slip one stitch as if to knit, slip another stitch as if to knit. Insert left-hand needle into front of these 2 stitches and knit them together
WS: Slip one stitch as if to purl, slip another stitch as if to purl. Slip these stitches back to the left-hand needle and purl stitches together through the back loop

C2 Over 1 Right (2/1 RC)
SL1 to CN, hold in back.
K2, K1 from CN

C2 Over 1 Left (2/1 LC)
SL2 to CN, hold in front.
K, K2 from CN

C2 Over 1 Right P (2/1 LPC)
SL1 to CN, hold in front.
K2, P1 from CN

C2 Over 1 Left P (2/1 RPC)
SL2 to CN, hold in front.
P1, K2 from CN

C2 Over 3 Right (2/3 RC)
SL3 to CN, hold in back.
K2, then K3 from CN

...to smile.

Abbreviations

BO	bind off	LH	left hand	Rev St st	reverse stockinette stitch	St st	stockinette stitch
cn	cable needle	M	marker			st(s)	stitch(es)
CC	contrast color	M1	make one stitch	RH	right hand	TBL	through back loop
CDD	centered double dec	M1L	make one left-leaning stitch	rnd(s)	round(s)	TFL	through front loop
CO	cast on	M1R	make one right-leaning stitch	RS	right side	tog	together
cont	continue			Sk	skip	W&T	wrap & turn (see specific instructions in pattern)
dec	decrease(es)	MC	main color	Sk2p	sl 1, k2tog, pass slipped stitch over k2tog: 2 sts dec		
DPN(s)	double pointed needle(s)	P	purl			WE	work even
EOR	every other row	P2tog	purl 2 sts together	SKP	sl, k, psso: 1 st dec	WS	wrong side
inc	increase	PM	place marker	SL	slip	WYIB	with yarn in back
K	knit	PFB	purl into the front and back of stitch	SM	slip marker	WYIF	with yarn in front
K2tog	knit two sts together			SSK	sl, sl, k these 2 sts tog	YO	yarn over
KFB	knit into the front and back of stitch	PSSO	pass slipped stitch over	SSP	sl, sl, p these 2 sts tog tbl		
K-wise	knitwise	PU	pick up	SSSK	sl, sl, sl, k these 3 sts tog		
		P-wise	purlwise				
		rep	repeat				

Knit Picks yarn is both luxe and affordable—a seeming contradiction trounced! But it's not just about the pretty colors; we also care deeply about fiber quality and fair labor practices, leaving you with a gorgeously reliable product you'll turn to time and time again.

THIS COLLECTION FEATURES

Aloft
Lace Weight
72% Super Kid Mohair, 28% Silk

Alpaca Cloud
Fingering Weight
100% Superfine Alpaca

Andean Treasure
Sport Weight
100% Baby Alpaca

The Big Cozy
Super Bulky Weight
55% Superfine Alpaca, 45% Peruvian Highland Wool

Brava
Worsted Weight
100% Premium Acrylic

Color Mist
Worsted Weight
75% Pima Cotton, 25% Acrylic

Comfy
Worsted Weight
75% Pima Cotton, 25% Acrylic

Shimmer
Bulky Weight
70% Baby Alpaca, 30% Mulberry Silk

Simply Alpaca
Aran Weight
100% Superfine Alpaca

Stroll
Fingering Weight
75% Fine Superwash Merino Wool, 25% Nylon

Swish
Worsted Weight
100% Superwash Merino Wool

Wonderfluff
Bulky Weight
70% Baby Alpaca, 7% Merino, 23% Nylon

View these beautiful yarns and more at www.KnitPicks.com